Sir Richard Branson
The Autobiography

RICHARD BRANSON

Level 6

Retold by Karen Holmes
Series Editors: Andy Hopkins and Jocelyn Potter

Pearson Education Limited
Edinburgh Gate, Harlow,
Essex CM20 2JE, England
and Associated Companies throughout the world.

ISBN 0 582 51224 7

First published in Great Britain in 1998 by Virgin Books Ltd
Under the title *Losing My Virginity*
This adaptation first published by Penguin Books 2002

1 3 5 7 9 10 8 6 4 2

Copyright © Richard Branson 1998

Richard Branson hereby asserts his moral right to be identified
as author of this work in accordance with sections 77 and 78
of the Copyright Designs and Patents Act, 1988.

Typeset by Ferdinand Pageworks, London
Set in 11/14pt Bembo
Reproduction by Spectrum Colour, Ipswich
Printed in Spain by Mateu Cromo, S. A. Pinto (Madrid)

Published by Pearson Education Limited in association with
Penguin Books Ltd, both companies being subsidiaries of Pearson Plc

For a complete list of the titles available in the Penguin Readers series please write to your local
Pearson Education office or to: Marketing Department, Penguin Longman Publishing,
80 Strand, London WC2R 0RL.

Contents

Introduction

Later, it became apparent to me that business could be creative … you want to create something you are proud of. That has always been my philosophy of business. I can honestly say that I have never gone into any business just to make money. A business has to involve you; it has to be fun, and it has to exercise your creative instincts.

Virgin Atlantic, Virgin Music, Virgin Radio, Virgin Cola … From records to soft drinks, flights to financial services, the Virgin name has dominated since the 1980s.

When Richard Branson was still at school, he began to use the skills that have made him one of the world's leading businessmen. His search for success, and love of challenge, have brought him wealth and fame. They have also led him into battle with major organizations like British Airways, and driven him to risk his life in hot-air balloons.

In this book, Branson tells his own story and examines the motives for his actions in both his business and personal lives. With great honesty he describes his battle to create Virgin, the excitement of building new businesses, and his grief when his plans went wrong. His belief that business can and should be fun is illustrated on every page.

Chapter 1 'You will either go to prison or become a millionaire.' 1950–1967

Marrakech, Morocco, 5.30 a.m.: I woke before Joan and sat up in bed. I still hadn't written to Holly and Sam, so I tore a page out of my notebook and wrote them a letter in case I didn't return. I told them how much I loved them and their mother, and I asked them to be strong.

I folded the letter and put it in my pocket. Dressed and ready, I lay down beside Joan. Holly and Sam climbed into the bed between us. Then Sam left to see the balloon in which I hoped to fly around the world.

10.15 a.m.: We had done all the checks, and were ready to go. I kissed Joan, Holly and Sam one last time. I was amazed at Joan's strength. Holly had been at my side for the last four days and she appeared totally in control of the situation. I thought Sam was as well, but then he burst into tears. I almost started crying with him.

I ran across to kiss Mum and Dad goodbye. Mum pressed a letter into my hand. 'Open it after six days,' she said. I silently hoped we would last that long.

11.19 a.m.: Ten, nine, eight, seven, six, five ... Per Lindstrand, a very experienced balloonist, counted down and I concentrated on working the cameras. The third member of our team was Alex Ritchie, the brilliant engineer who designed the balloon. We rose up and away, and we passed over Marrakech.

Apart from a couple of small dramas concerning the fuel tanks and our route over Algeria, we flew quietly for the rest of the day. But just after 6 p.m., from 9,000 metres, the balloon started to lose height.

'What's the matter?' I asked.

'I don't know,' Per replied.

It was getting dark and the balloon continued to fall. We dropped more than 600 metres in one minute; another 600 metres the next. Soon we were only a few hundred metres above the ground, somewhere over the Atlas Mountains in darkness, and heading for a horrible crash-landing.

Per threw one of the fuel tanks over the side to get rid of some weight. The balloon stopped falling, then began to rise. In ten minutes, we were up past 1,000 metres and the balloon was heading back into the night sky. I promised myself that if I escaped from this flight with my life, I would never do it again.

Throughout the night we fought to keep control of the balloon. One of the remaining fuel tanks leaked and we lost a lot of fuel. As dawn approached, we prepared to land in the Algerian desert.

The bare earth was red and rocky, as empty as the surface of Mars, but within minutes there were signs of life. A group of Berbers came out from behind the rocks. Then two helicopters landed close by, throwing up clouds of dust. Soon we were surrounded by soldiers holding guns, apparently unsure where to point them. I looked at the balloon and saw it through their eyes. The sides were covered with signs for Virgin Atlantic, Virgin Direct, Virgin Territory and Virgin Cola. I repeated my promise that I would never attempt this again. But I knew that as soon as I was home and had talked to other balloonists, I would agree to try one last time.

The two questions I am most often asked are, 'Why do you risk your life ballooning?' and 'Where is the Virgin Group going?' I knew that I would attempt another balloon flight because it is one of the few remaining great challenges. As soon as I stop thinking about the terrors of each flight, I feel confident that we can learn from our mistakes and achieve the next one safely.

The wider question about the future of the Virgin Group is impossible to answer. I have written this book to show how we made Virgin what it is today. If you read it carefully you will, I hope, understand what our vision for the Virgin Group is, and you will see where I am going. This book is the first part of my autobiography. It covers the first forty-three years of my life. The book ends in January 1993 – the year after I was forced to sell Virgin Music – when Virgin Atlantic had its extraordinary victory over British Airways. This was an important point in Virgin's history: for the first time in my life, I had money to spend; we had lots of dreams and I was free to see what we could create at Virgin. How we put these dreams into practice will be the material for the next book.

◆

I cannot remember a moment in my life when I have not felt the love of my family. We were a family that would have killed for each other – and we still are. My mother, Eve, was always full of energy. My father was rather quieter, but they both had a love of adventure.

My parents always treated my two sisters, Lindi and Vanessa, and me as equals; our opinions were just as important as theirs. We lived in a village called Shamley Green in Surrey. I was three years older than Lindi, and nine years older than Vanessa. My parents had very little money during our childhood.

My best friend, Nik Powell, lived near us. He was a quiet boy with straight black hair and black eyes. Soon we started doing everything together: climbing trees, riding bikes, shooting rabbits, and hiding under Lindi's bed to grab her ankle when she turned out the light. I can't remember a time when Nik and I weren't friends.

At home Mum was always thinking of ways to make money. We never had a television and I don't think my parents ever listened to the radio. Mum made wooden boxes and wastepaper bins which she sold to shops. Eventually she began supplying Harrods with her boxes.

There was a great sense of teamwork within our family. Whenever we were near Mum, we had to be busy. If we tried to escape by saying that we had something else to do, we were firmly told we were selfish. As a result we grew up with a clear priority of considering other people first.

When we were eight years old, Nik and I were separated when I was sent away to Scaitcliffe School. My father had gone away to school at the same age, and his father before him. It was the traditional way for a boy from my background to be educated, to encourage independence, but I hated being away from home.

In my third week at Scaitcliffe, I was called to the headmaster's study and told that I had broken a rule. I had to bend down and I was beaten across my bottom six times.

'Branson,' the headmaster said, 'say, "Thank you, sir."'

I couldn't believe my ears. Thank him for what?

'Branson.' The headmaster lifted up his stick. 'I'm warning you.'

'Thank you . . . sir.'

'You're going to be trouble, Branson.'

'Yes, sir. I mean, no, sir.'

I was always in trouble. Aged eight, I still couldn't read. In fact, I was dyslexic and short-sighted. My dyslexia was a problem throughout my school life. Now, although my spelling is sometimes poor, I have managed to overcome the worst of my difficulties by training myself to concentrate. Perhaps my early problems with dyslexia made me trust my instincts. When someone sends me a written proposal, rather than concentrating on detailed facts and figures, I find that my imagination understands and expands on what I read.

4

I moved to Stowe, a big school in Buckinghamshire for over 800 boys, in 1963. It was an old-fashioned place. To be successful there, you had to be good at games. I was at a disadvantage since I had hurt my knee when I was younger and couldn't run. I couldn't cope with my studies, either. It was an unenviable position.

Every afternoon I escaped to the library and started writing a novel. I wrote colourful sexual stories about a young boy who couldn't play sports because of a knee injury. He was made love to expertly by the young Scandinavian school nurse. She crept up behind him when he was working. Sadly for me, whatever sexual dreams I had, there were no girls anywhere near Stowe, and the school nurse was sixty years old.

As I sat in the library, I became aware of another regular visitor, Jonathan Holland-Gems. In comparison with most of the boys at Stowe, Jonny was extremely smart and knew a lot about the arts. His parents knew writers and journalists, and my interest in the world of newspapers began to grow.

One Easter holiday, I decided to follow my mother's example and make some money by growing Christmas trees. We had just moved to Tanyards Farm, which was a big old building with some land. I went round to talk to Nik about the plan. We would plant 400 Christmas trees in the field. By the Christmas after next, they would be more than a metre high and we could sell them. Nik and I agreed to do the work together, and share the profits equally.

That Easter we planted 400 seeds in the field above Tanyards Farm. We worked out that if they all grew to nearly two metres, we would make £2 a tree, a total of £800, compared with our initial investment of just £5 for the seeds. In the following summer holiday, we went to investigate our trees. There were one or two tiny stems above ground, but rabbits had eaten the rest. We shot a lot of the rabbits and sold them to the local butcher for five pence each, but it wasn't the £800 we had planned.

During January and February 1966, Jonny and I began to talk about how to change the school rules. I have always thought that rules are meant to be broken, and Stowe had as many rules as the army. We had to dress up as soldiers and march around with old guns, and we had to go to church on Sundays. We were fifteen years old, but we believed that we could make a difference. My parents had brought me up to think that we could all change the world, so when I looked at how Stowe was run I felt sure I could do it better.

The headmaster suggested that I present my views in the school magazine, but Jonny and I wanted to set up an alternative magazine with a fresh attitude. We wanted to protest against physical punishment, and having to go to church and games. All these ideas were much too 'revolutionary' for the school magazine. We then thought about linking up with other schools that had similar rules. Gradually the idea of an interschool magazine developed.

I wrote a list of 250 politicians and, from the phone book, a list of possible advertisers. I also wrote to the retailer WH Smith asking whether they would sell the magazine. So with contributors, advertisers, distributors and costs all in place – at least on paper – I wrote my first business plan.

The numbers looked too small to work, so Jonny and I decided to involve more schools, colleges and universities: it would open up the magazine to more people, and encourage advertisers. We decided on the name *Student*, which seemed a good one since at the time there was a great deal of talk about 'student power'. My mother lent me £4 for telephone calls and letters, and Jonny's father arranged for notepaper with *STUDENT* – THE MAGAZINE FOR BRITAIN'S YOUTH printed across the top with the symbol of a rising sun. We began writing to all the contributors and possible advertisers.

There was so much to organize. I set up an office in my study at school and asked the headmaster for a telephone in my room – he, unsurprisingly, refused. As a result I had to make telephone calls from a call box, but I quickly discovered a useful trick: if I called the operator and told her that the machine had taken my money, but my call hadn't been connected, I got a free call. Even better, the operator sounded like a secretary: 'I have Mr Branson for you.'

Most businesses rejected the idea of paying for advertising in an unpublished magazine, but gradually I found ways to attract their attention. I would call National Westminster Bank and tell them that Lloyds Bank had just agreed to pay for a full-page advertisement; would they like to advertise next to Lloyds? *Student* would be Britain's biggest magazine for young people, I added. I called Coca-Cola and told them that Pepsi had just booked a big advertisement, but that the back page was still free. Another trick was to ask a question that they couldn't easily deny: 'Are you interested in attracting the best school-leavers and university graduates to work in your company? Then we're publishing just the magazine for you . . .'

To avoid the operator coming back on the line to cut me off, I learnt how to say all this in five minutes. My voice was deep and nobody guessed that they were talking to a fifteen-year-old schoolboy standing in a public telephone box. I gave my address at Shamley Green, and when I wrote letters I posted them to my parents, who asked an old friend in the village to type them.

My schoolwork was going from bad to worse, but I was becoming very confident. If I had been five or six years older, the impossibility of trying to sell advertising to major companies, in a magazine that did not yet exist, run by two schoolboys, would have prevented me from picking up the phone. But I was too young to think about failure.

During the holidays I told Nik about *Student*. He was equally excited and agreed to help distribute it at his school. He would also try to find contributors. Nik recognized that *Student* was really my and Jonny's creation, but he was as enthusiastic as we were. We felt we could do anything.

Despite my enthusiasm, it took a long time to find any advertisers to take space in *Student*. Jonny and I sent letters out all summer term, and continued in the holidays and through the following autumn term. We had been working on *Student* for over a year, and all we had were letters of support from various teachers, and some promises to contribute from politicians, but no advertisements or articles. Then we had our first successes: we received our first article and a £250 cheque for an advertisement. *Student* was finally becoming a real magazine.

The other thing that became a reality was sex. I had a number of girlfriends during the holidays and came closer and closer to losing my virginity at parties, when the lights went out and everyone lay around on cushions. But my first real girlfriend was Rudi, a Dutch 'revolutionary', and in my last term I invited her to Stowe. She moved into the school grounds and secretly put up her tent in the middle of the wood. For one wonderful week I crept out every night and walked past the lake to the woods, where Rudi would be smoking marijuana and cooking. We lay under the stars and talked about how we would change the world. Rudi was very interested in world politics. She became *Student*'s grandly titled 'Dutch overseas reporter' and wrote some powerful pieces about the revolutionary German Baader Meinhof gang.

After dropping all subjects except ancient history, I had even more time for *Student* magazine. Soon Jonny and I were regularly taking the train to London to interview people. I was too interested in *Student* to care about examinations. I just wanted to leave Stowe and start life as a journalist in London.

When I left Stowe in 1967, aged almost seventeen, my headmaster's last words to me were: 'Congratulations, Branson. I predict that you will either go to prison or become a millionaire.'

The first issue of *Student* was published in January 1968.

Chapter 2   Virgins at business 1967–1970

At the end of the summer term of 1967, Jonny and I moved into the basement of his parents' house in Connaught Square, in London. The number of people involved with *Student* began to grow. Jonny and I went to nightclubs to meet girls. Sometimes we could persuade them to come back to the flat, 'for coffee'. If they stayed the night, the next morning we would try to persuade them to help us. For some reason, they often agreed.

The news spread: old friends came from school; friends of friends, or people who had read the magazine, wanted to be involved. We all worked for no money, eating whatever was in the fridge and going out for cheap meals.

I never really worried about how much profit *Student* made: I just wanted to have enough cash to produce the next issue and pay our bills. The more copies we sold, the more publicity we would get and the more advertising we would attract.

My ambition to be a journalist was replaced by the need to keep the magazine going. Jonny ran the editorial side while I ran the business, sold advertising space and argued with the printers. I was becoming a businessman. I certainly didn't regard myself as one. Businessmen were middle-aged men in the City* who only thought about making money. Of course, we wanted to make money on *Student* too – we needed money to survive. But it was more of a creative project than a money-making one.

Later, it became apparent to me that business could be creative. If you publish a magazine, you are trying to create something that is original, that will last and serve a useful purpose. Above all, you want to create something you are proud of. That has always been my philosophy of business. I can honestly say that I have never gone into any business just to make

* the City: London's financial centre.

9

money. A business has to involve you; it has to be fun, and it has to exercise your creative instincts.

Despite our efforts, *Student* wasn't making money. I began to think of ways to develop the magazine and the *Student* name in other directions: a *Student* conference, a *Student* travel company, a *Student* accommodation agency. I saw *Student* as the beginning of a whole range of services, a name that people would recognize as having certain key values. I wanted to explore the concept of *Student* to see where it would lead. In this way I was a little removed from the rest of my friends, who concentrated on the magazine and the student politics they wanted to write about.

Soon a number of journalists from the national papers came to interview me. We developed a guaranteed way of impressing them. I sat at my desk, the telephone at my elbow.

'Great to meet you. Take a seat,' I would say, waving the journalist down into the chair opposite me. Then the telephone would ring.

'Can someone take that, please?' I would ask. 'Now –' I turned my attention to the journalist '– what do you want to know about *Student*?'

'It's Ted Heath for you, Richard,' Tony would call across. Edward Heath was leader of the government at the time.

'I'll call him back,' I'd say over my shoulder.

By this time the journalist was turning round to watch Tony tell Ted Heath that he was sorry, but Richard was in a meeting and he'd call him back. Then the telephone would ring again, and Tony would pick it up.

'David Bailey for you, Richard.' David Bailey was a world-famous photographer.

'I'll call him back, but will you ask if he can change that lunch date? I've got to be in Paris. OK –' I'd flash an apologetic grin at the journalist '– now, what do you want to know?'

'I just wanted to ask you –'

The telephone rang again.

'I'm sorry to interrupt,' Tony would apologize, 'but it's Mick Jagger for you and he says it's urgent.'

'Please excuse me for a minute,' I'd say, picking up the phone. 'Mick, hello. Fine thanks, and you? Really? An interview? Yes, that sounds great . . .'

And I would continue like this until Jonny couldn't stop laughing in the telephone box opposite.

'I'm sorry,' I'd say to the journalist. 'Something's happened and we've got to go. Have we finished?'

Journalists were deceived by our trick. 'An amazing number of top-class contributors,' said the *Observer*, while the *Daily Telegraph* said, 'It seems . . . that *Student*, the publication that has attracted a lot of well-known writers, will become one of the best-selling magazines in the country.'

♦

In autumn 1968, we moved to 44 Albion Street, just round the corner from Connaught Square. Jonny left to go back to school. Without him, *Student* almost fell to pieces. There was too much for me to do, and I didn't trust anybody else to help. After a few weeks, I asked Nik to join me.

With Nik's arrival, *Student* recovered. He started controlling the cash. Instead of having a large biscuit tin full of money which anyone could use for food, drink or marijuana, Nik used our bank account properly. He started writing cheques and checking the bank statements.

By now most of the people working with *Student* were nineteen or twenty. We talked about free love and we practised it. I installed a large bed on the top floor, with a telephone running to it. Some days I did all my business from bed.

I had a short relationship with Debbie, one of the girls working on the magazine. One day she told me she was

11

pregnant. We were both very shocked; we realized that we couldn't cope with a baby. Debbie decided that she wanted an abortion. After a few telephone calls it was clear that this would be very difficult to arrange. The National Health Service would not carry out an abortion unless Debbie had psychological or medical problems. When we tried to find a private doctor, we found it would cost over £400 – money we didn't have. I finally found a doctor in Birmingham who said she would arrange the operation for £50.

Debbie and I realized that there must be thousands of young people who faced the same problem and couldn't get help. It would be much better if there was one telephone number you could ring to find the right doctor. Unwanted pregnancies were not the only problem. What could you do if you needed psychological help, or had a sexual disease but were scared of admitting it to your family doctor? Or if you ran away and had nowhere to live?

GIVE US YOUR HEADACHES offered the Student Advisory Centre. We handed out leaflets along Oxford Street and advertised in *Student*. Soon the calls started coming in. A number of doctors, both in the National Health Service and private practice, agreed to give their services free or very cheaply and we built up a network of professionals who would help.

The Student Advisory Centre began to take up more time than *Student* magazine. I would talk to people who wanted to kill themselves at three in the morning. I would advise pregnant girls about the nicest doctor they could see, and write to people who were afraid that they had caught a sexual disease. In the remaining time, I was trying to run the magazine.

◆

One day in 1970 I came back to my desk and found that Nik had been sitting there. By mistake he had left a letter which he was writing to the staff. He wanted to take editorial and financial control of *Student* and let the staff jointly run the magazine. I would just be part of the team. I was shocked. I felt that Nik – my best friend – was betraying me.

I looked around at everyone working. They all had their heads bent down over their desks. I wondered how many of them were part of this plan. I put the letter in my pocket. When Nik came back I stood up.

'Nik,' I said, 'will you come outside for a quick chat?'

I decided to use psychology to get through the crisis. If Nik already had support from the ten other people, it would be difficult for me to stop them. But if they were undecided, I could divide Nik from the rest of them and cut him out. I had to put friendship to one side, and get rid of this challenge.

'Nik,' I said, as we walked down the street, 'a number of people have told me that they're unhappy with your plans. They don't like the idea but they're too scared to tell you.'

Nik looked shocked.

'I think that we should remain friends,' I went on, 'but I don't think you should stay here any more.'

Nik looked down at his feet. 'I'm sorry, Ricky,' he said. 'It just seemed a better way to organize ourselves . . .'

'I'm sorry too, Nik.' I folded my arms and looked straight at him.

Nik left that day. I told everyone that we had disagreed over how to run *Student*, and they were free to leave or stay. They all decided to stay with me.

This was the first real disagreement I ever had. Although I felt very upset, I knew I had to face it. I hate criticising people who work with me, and I try to avoid doing so. I admit this is a weakness, but I am simply unable to cope with it.

Nik was my best friend and I hoped that he would remain so. When I was next down in Shamley Green I went round to see him and found him eating one of his mum's puddings. We sat down together and finished it.

♦

Everyone who came in to chat or work for us spent a lot of time listening to music. There was a tremendous excitement about music: it was political, it expressed young people's dreams of changing the world. People who would never spend two pounds on a meal wouldn't hesitate to spend two pounds on the latest Bob Dylan album.

I thought about the high cost of records and the people who bought *Student* magazine, and wondered whether we could advertise and sell cheap records through the magazine. The first advertisement for mail-order records appeared in the final issue. Without Nik to manage *Student*'s distribution, it was failing, but the offer of cheap records brought in a lot of enquiries and more cash than we had ever seen before.

We decided to find another name for the mail-order business: a name that would appeal not just to students. We sat around trying to choose a good one. One of the girls leant forward. 'I know,' she said. 'What about "Virgin"? We're complete virgins at business.'

'And there aren't many virgins around here,' laughed another girl. 'It would be nice to have one here even if it is just a name.'

'Great,' I decided immediately. 'It's Virgin.'

Chapter 3 'You'd better come with me. I'm arresting you.' 1970–1971

And so we became Virgin. Our ideas were correct: students spent a lot of money on records and they didn't like spending £1.99 at WH Smith when they could buy them from Virgin for £1.75.

14

We gave out leaflets about Virgin Mail Order Records along Oxford Street and outside concerts, and the number of orders increased. One of the best things about mail order was that the customers sent their money in first: this provided the capital for us to buy the records.

As Virgin Mail Order grew, I tried to sell *Student* to another magazine group. IPC Magazines were interested, and we had long negotiations which ended in a meeting where they asked me to continue as editor. I agreed to do so, but then made the mistake of telling them my future plans for *Student*. I felt that banks treated students badly, and I wanted to set up a cheap student bank; I wanted to open nightclubs and hotels for students; I wanted to offer them good travel, like student trains or even a student airline. The IPC executives thought that I was crazy. They decided they didn't want a madman as editor of *Student*, and decided not to buy it. *Student* died a quiet death, and my plans for the future were forgotten for the moment.

I also forgot my disagreement with Nik, and offered him 40 per cent of the newly formed Virgin Mail Order Records company if he came to work with me. He agreed immediately. We never negotiated over the 60–40 split. I think we both felt that it was a fair reflection of what we would each put into the business.

Although Nik was not a trained financial manager, he was careful with money. He also set an example to us: he never spent money, so why should any of us? He never washed his clothes, so why should anyone else? He saved every penny; he always turned lights off when he left a room, and he handled our bills with great skill.

Throughout 1970 Virgin Mail Order Records did well. Then, in January 1971, we were almost ruined by something entirely out of our control: the Post Office workers went on strike. People couldn't send us cheques; we couldn't send out records. We had to do something.

Nik and I decided to open a shop to continue selling the records. We wanted the Virgin Records shop to be a place where people could meet and listen to music; where they didn't have to run in, buy a record and leave. People are more serious about music than many other things in life. It is part of the way they define themselves, like the cars they drive, the films they watch and the clothes they wear.

Virgin's first record shop had to include all these ways in which music fitted into people's lives. By exploring this, we created the model for what Virgin later became. We wanted to understand our customers and to be cheaper than other shops. This was a lot to achieve, but if people bought more records it would compensate for the money which we spent on creating the atmosphere, and the profits we gave up by selling cheaply.

Nik and I decided that the cheaper end of Oxford Street would be the best site. We knew we couldn't rely on people knowing about the Virgin Records shop and making a special trip to buy a record, so we had to attract people passing by. At the exact point where we counted the most people walking along the street, we started looking for an empty property. We saw a shoe shop with a stairway leading up to an empty first floor, so we went upstairs.

'What are you doing?' a voice called up to us.

'We want to set up a record shop,' we said. We came back down the stairs and found the owner of the shoe shop in front of us.

'You'll never pay the rent,' he said.

'No, you're right,' I said. 'We can't afford any rent. But we'll attract lots of people past your window and they'll all buy your shoes.'

He agreed that we could occupy the first floor for no rent until somebody else wanted it. Within five days we had built shelves, put piles of cushions on the floor and set up a till. The first Virgin Records shop was ready for business.

The day before the opening, we handed out leaflets along Oxford Street offering cheap records. On the first day, a Monday, a queue over a hundred metres long formed outside.

At the end of the day I took the money to the bank. I found the shoe-shop owner outside the shop.

'How's business?' I asked, trying to hide the heavy bag of cash I was carrying.

He looked at me and then at his shop window, which was still full of unsold shoes. 'Fine,' he said firmly. 'Couldn't be better.'

◆

As a record retailer, Virgin would succeed as long as there were bands whose records people wanted to buy. But the real way to make money in the record industry was as a record company.

At first, Nik and I concentrated on building up the shop. We continued to find different ways to welcome our customers. We offered them free copies of music magazines to read, and free coffee to drink. We let them stay as long as they liked. Soon people seemed to think that the same album by Bob Dylan had greater value if they bought it at Virgin rather than another retailer like Boots. With loyal customers, Virgin's reputation began to grow.

At the other end of the business from buying records – the recording studios – I heard that conditions were very formal. Bands had to arrive at a certain time, bring their own equipment and set it up, then leave at a certain time and take all their equipment with them. I thought that the best environment for making records would be a big, comfortable house where a band could stay for weeks and record whenever they felt like it. So during 1971 I started looking for a country house that I could turn into a recording studio.

I went to see one property with Tom Newman, one of the first people to join the Virgin Mail Order company. He was a singer who had already made a couple of records, but was more interested in setting up a recording studio. We saw a beautiful seventeenth-century manor house at Shipton-on-Cherwell, eight kilometres north of Oxford. We walked around the outside of the house and both realized that this would be perfect.

With a loan from the bank, and some help from my family, I raised the money to buy the Manor. Tom Newman and his friend Phil Newell immediately started developing part of the Manor into a recording studio. We both wanted the latest equipment, so that everything was as good as the best studio in London.

Throughout the spring of 1971, Virgin Mail Order attracted many more customers. But although the company was growing, we were losing money. We sold records cheaply and, by the time we had spent money on the telephone calls to order them, paid for the postage, the staff and the shops, we weren't making a profit. Sometimes our customers pretended that they hadn't received the records, so we would have to send out a second copy, and often a third and fourth. Soon we owed the bank £15,000.

I received an order from Belgium for a large number of records. I went to the record companies that published those records and bought them without paying the purchase tax which we had to pay on records sold in the UK. Then I borrowed a van and drove to Dover to take the ferry to France and drive to Belgium. Some papers were stamped at Dover to confirm that the records had been exported, but when I arrived at Calais I was asked for another document to prove that I wasn't going to sell them in France. The British and French both charged purchase tax on records, while Belgium charged nothing. I did not have this document and was forced to go back to Dover on the ferry, with the records still in my van.

As I drove back to London, I realized that I was carrying a vanload of records that had apparently been exported. I even had a customs stamp to prove it. I could sell them either by mail order or at the Virgin shop and make about £5,000 profit. Two or three more trips like this and we would be out of debt.

It was a criminal plan and I was breaking the law. But I had broken the rules before. In those days I felt I could do no wrong and that, even if I did, I wouldn't be caught. I was only twenty years old and the normal everyday rules didn't seem to apply to me. I was also falling in love with a beautiful American girl called Kristen Tomassi.

I met Kristen at the Manor. She had come to England for a holiday and met a musician who was working there. We drove back to London in separate cars. Kristen was with her boyfriend and I was by myself. As I drove along, I wrote a note on a piece of paper asking her to call me at seven o'clock. I waited until we reached some traffic lights, then jumped out and ran up to their car. I tapped on Kristen's window and she rolled it down.

'I just wanted to say goodbye,' I said, leaning in to kiss her cheek. 'Have a good trip back to the States.'

As I said this, I secretly put my hand inside the car and pushed my note into her left hand. When Kristen's fingers closed round mine, I passed her the note. I smiled across at the boyfriend.

'Hope the recording went well,' I said to him.

At seven o'clock, the phone rang. It was Kristen. 'I'm calling from a payphone,' she said. 'I didn't want John to hear.'

'Can you catch a taxi?' I asked. 'Come round and see me.' Kristen came round and our love affair began.

The next morning I was due to make my final trip to Dover, pretending to export records. By this time I had made three trips and £12,000 profit. I loaded up the van with records once again and set off. This time, after my papers were stamped I didn't even bother going on the ferry, but simply drove around the dock and went back to London. I was anxious to make sure that Kristen was still there.

While Kristen and I spent the rest of the day in bed, the

customs officers were planning to search Virgin. It never occurred to me that I wasn't the only person who avoided paying tax. Many larger record shops were doing it, and they were more clever than I was. I was simply putting records that should be exported in our Virgin Records shop on Oxford Street and the new shop in Liverpool, which was due to open the next week. The big operators were distributing their illegally 'exported' records across the country.

The telephone rang at around midnight. The caller refused to give his name, but he warned me that my trips to Europe had been noticed and I was going to be searched. He said that if I bought a sun lamp from a chemist's shop and shone it on the records that I had bought from EMI, I would find a brightly coloured E stamped on all the ones that should have been exported to Belgium.

I called Nik and Tony, and rushed out to buy two sun lamps from a late-night chemist. We met and started pulling records out of their covers. The awful truth was revealed: an E shone up at us from all the records we had bought from EMI for export. We began carrying piles of records into the van. We then made a terrible mistake: we assumed that the officials would just search the place where we stored the records. We therefore drove all the records round to the Oxford Street shop and put them on the shelves to be sold.

Next morning, Kristen and I walked to work. But before we reached my office there was a knock on the door. I opened it, and found seven or eight men in brown coats. 'Are you Richard Branson?' they said. 'We're Customs officers and we've come to inspect your stock.'

They began to check all the records with their own sun lamp and grew increasingly worried when they couldn't find any marked records. I enjoyed their confusion, and hoped that our plan would succeed. I didn't realize that they were searching our shops in Oxford Street and Liverpool at the same time and finding hundreds of marked records.

'All right.' One of the officers put down the telephone. 'They've found them. You'd better come with me. I'm arresting you.'

I couldn't believe it. I had always thought that only criminals were arrested; I hadn't thought that I had become one. I had been stealing money from Customs.

I spent that night in a cell lying on a bare bed with one old blanket. The first part of my Stowe headmaster's prediction had come true: I was in prison.

That night was one of the best things that has ever happened to me. As I lay in the cell, I promised that I would never again do anything that could put me in prison, or do any kind of business deal that would embarrass me. Since that night, there have been times when I could have taken a bribe, or could have offered one. But I have never been tempted to break my promise. My parents had always told me that the most important thing in life is your reputation: you may be rich, but if you lose your good name you'll never be happy.

The next morning, Mum met me at the court. She told the judge that she would offer Tanyards Farm, her home, as security for my release until the case was heard. We stared at each other across the court and both started crying. The trust that my family had in me had to be repaid.

Over the summer I faced the problem and kept a clear head. I was sorry; I wouldn't do it again. I negotiated a deal with the Customs office. The tax authorities in the UK are more interested in getting their money than in expensive court cases. On 18 August 1971 I agreed to pay £15,000 immediately, and £45,000 over the next three years. If I paid these sums, I would avoid a criminal record. But if I failed to pay, I would be rearrested and taken to court.

Since there was limited growth left in the mail-order business, we concentrated on expanding the record shops. We knew we had to sell more records. We also wanted to attract important musicians like Cat Stevens or Paul McCartney to record at the Manor, and set up a record company. We didn't know that our first fortune was quietly coming up the road to the Manor inside another van. This time it was not carrying records, but bringing a young musician and his sister. Their names were Mike and Sally Oldfield.

Chapter 4 'It's called *Tubular Bells* ...' 1971–1973

Before the postal strike nearly ruined us in January 1971, someone with a South African accent walked into my office and introduced himself as my cousin. Simon Draper had graduated from Natal University and come to London with just £100. He was thinking of doing a higher degree, but meanwhile he was looking for a job.

Simon loved music. It seemed that he had listened to every record released by every band. He didn't just enjoy the latest Doors album: he understood what they were doing and how they had developed from their previous album. I persuaded Simon to be the record buyer for the Virgin Records shop and the Virgin mail-order list. There was no awkward salary negotiation since everyone at Virgin was paid the same – £20 per week. I let him get on with the job for the first few months.

While Nik managed the costs of the mail-order business and the Virgin Records shops, Simon chose the records for both. Simon's taste in music quickly became the single most important quality of Virgin. I didn't know what to promote, but Simon was full of wonderful plans to bring in unknown foreign albums that were unavailable elsewhere. He started importing records from the US, flying them in to beat the competition.

As well as imports, we also made a lot of money by dealing in records which had gone out of stock and were being sold off by the record company. Since we operated a mail-order business, we had hundreds of letters every day asking for special recordings. We therefore knew what people wanted, and it was quite simple for us to buy popular records cheaply and sell them.

Nik and I began a programme of serious growth. Towards the end of 1971 and throughout 1972 we aimed to open a shop every month. By Christmas 1972 we had fourteen record shops: several in London and one in every big city across the country. As we opened these shops, we learnt lessons that helped us in the future. We always looked for property at the cheaper end of the high street, where we could attract shoppers without paying a high rent. We also asked local teenagers where the best place for a record shop would be – 130 Notting Hill Gate became one of the best Virgin shops.

We knew we were successful when people started coming up to London just to go to a Virgin Records shop. If we could have sold marijuana, we would have done. In fact, I suspect that some of the staff did. Selling records, chatting to the customers, recommending which music to buy, going to pubs and clubs to hear more bands play: it became a way of life.

When we opened our Virgin Records shop in Bold Street, Liverpool, in March 1972, I proudly saw that we took £10,000 in the first week. A week later the figure was £7,000, and the following week it was down to £3,000. By the middle of the summer it had dropped to £2,000 and I went up to see what was going wrong. The place was packed with people but nobody was buying anything. Everyone was having a good time, but nobody could get to the till and they were keeping other shoppers out of the store. The practice of treating our shops like clubs was out of control. For the next month we had someone at the door who gently warned people that they were going into a shop, not a

23

nightclub; we put in brighter lights and moved the counter and till nearer the window. It was difficult to maintain the shop's atmosphere and keep up profits but the figures eventually improved.

During 1972 Simon fell in love with a South American girl and told me he was leaving Virgin and going to live in Chile with her. The Manor was at last open for artists to record; there were twenty record shops, and the mail-order business was doing well. Simon had been working with me for a year and I suddenly realized how important he was. His choice in music had made Virgin shops the best place to buy records. I tried to persuade Simon to stay, but he was determined to leave. His girlfriend went to Chile first, and Simon planned to join her a month later. During that month he suddenly received a letter from her which broke off the relationship. He was very disappointed, but at the same time realized that his future lay in London rather than South America. We started to talk about our third dream: the Virgin record label.

If Virgin set up a record label, we could offer musicians somewhere to record (for which we could charge them). We could produce and release their records (from which we could make a profit). We also had a growing chain of shops where we could promote and sell their records (and make a profit).

Simon and I agreed that he would set up and run the new Virgin record label, Virgin Music. He would own 20 per cent of the company, which would be separate from the Virgin record shops. And the first person Simon and I wanted for the label was Mike Oldfield.

♦

In October 1971, Mike was working at the Manor, playing the guitar on another musician's recordings. He started chatting to Tom Newman, and one day gave him a tape of his own music. Tom listened to it and said it was brilliant. He helped Mike to approach some record companies, but they weren't interested.

A year later, Simon and I called Mike. To our delight he had still not signed up with anyone. He felt rejected by the record industry and was pleased that we wanted to release his music. I suggested that Mike should go back to the Manor and live there, and he and Tom Newman could work on his record.

It took Mike a long time to record what became *Tubular Bells*. It was a complicated set of recordings. Mike played over twenty different instruments and made over 2,300 different recordings before he was happy. Meanwhile we were still trying to rent out the Manor to any band we could find. Mike was often interrupted and had to clear his instruments out of the recording studio to make way for The Rolling Stones.

On 22 July 1972, Kristen and I were married at the tiny church of Shipton-on-Cherwell. I was just twenty-two and Kristen was twenty. We had known each other only since May the previous year.

Throughout the winter of 1972 and the spring of 1973, Mike Oldfield lived at the Manor and recorded *Tubular Bells*. We knew that it was extraordinary when we started selling *Tubular Bells* to the record industry. Simon took the recording along to the sales conference at Island Records, the company that was going to distribute the album. They had already listened to hours of music. Simon put on *Tubular Bells* and they listened to the whole of the first side. When it finished, they started to clap. Simon never again heard a roomful of experienced salesmen clap for a new record.

On 25 May 1973, Virgin Music released its first four albums: Mike Oldfield's *Tubular Bells*; *Flying Teapot* by Gong; *Manor Live*, a live recording from the Manor led by Elkie Brooks; and *The Faust Tapes* by Faust, a German band.

Faust won great praise in the newspapers, but it was *Tubular Bells* that really impressed people. They played it again and again. The biggest problem was persuading radio producers to put it in their programmes. At that time, three-minute records dominated radio music; there was no room for a 45-minute piece of music without words.

Then I invited John Peel for lunch. We had known each other since I had interviewed him for *Student* and he was the only person who played serious rock music on the radio. I put on *Tubular Bells* and he was amazed.

'I've never heard anything like it,' John finally said.

Later that week we listened to John Peel's voice on the radio. I was sitting with Mike Oldfield and everyone from Virgin.

'Tonight I'm not going to play a lot of records. I'm just going to play you one by a young musician called Mike Oldfield. It's his first record and it's called *Tubular Bells*. It's released by Virgin, a new record label, and it was recorded at Virgin's own studios in Oxfordshire. You'll never forget this.'

Thousands of people across the country listened to John Peel and respected his opinions. All the next day, the phones rang with orders from record shops for *Tubular Bells*. By August, it was number one in the album charts.* For the next fifteen years, whenever Mike Oldfield made an album it reached the top ten. *Tubular Bells* eventually sold over thirteen million copies, making it the eleventh-best-selling album ever made in Britain.

Although Virgin became a popular record label overnight, we were a tiny company with a staff of seven people. We couldn't distribute records to all the record shops across the country. We had two options. The first was to license our records to another larger record label. This would work only for fairly successful bands. The other company would give us an advance payment for the right to promote the record, distribute it and keep most of the profits. If the record earned more than the value of the advance payment, the record company would pay us a royalty, typically about 16 per cent.

* the charts: a list of best-selling records produced by retailers every week.

The second option was more risky. Virgin would pay another record label to manufacture and distribute the records when they were ordered by shops around the country. Virgin would promote its records and carry all the risk if the record failed. But we would have more of the profit if the record sold well.

We went to see Island Records. At first they refused to do a manufacturing and distribution deal. They appeared to be better placed than Virgin to promote the record. But Simon and I felt differently. We had fourteen Virgin shops across the country which could promote *Tubular Bells*. We also felt that we could do the promotion in the national and music press ourselves. Eventually Island agreed to the deal.

We became very rich as the sales of *Tubular Bells* went over a million copies. We grew into a major force in the record industry and eventually became the rival to Island Records. *Tubular Bells* still sells around the world today. Our belief that we could promote it ourselves made our first fortune.

The next step was to sell our records overseas. I flew to New York to see Ahmet Ertegun, the head of Atlantic Records and one of the most influential men in the entertainment business.

Ahmet was the grand old man of American music and I was twenty-three years old. I was shown into his office. Ahmet made it clear that he was very busy, but that he could spare fifteen minutes to agree the Mike Oldfield deal. He told me he was interested in Mike Oldfield because he was so original. He made me an offer of $180,000 and smiled at me encouragingly. I knew that he expected me to ask for more, and that we could agree on $200,000 within fifteen minutes. I shook my head. Ahmet smiled again and admitted that he too would have refused such an offer, but now his real offer was $200,000. That had to be his final offer. I allowed a silence to fall between us.

'What do you think?' Ahmet asked.

'I'm not going to tell you,' I said. 'But it's a lot more.'

27

That evening he offered to take me to a nightclub where we would have to agree a deal before we went home. As his car stopped outside my hotel, I saw that Ahmet was sitting in the back with two beautiful black girls. I thought that if he had provided such lovely company, then he must want *Tubular Bells* very badly. Surely he was going to offer over $500,000.

We stopped outside the nightclub and I followed Ahmet and the girls inside.

'Can I speak to you?' Ahmet took me to one side as we stood waiting for our table.

'Of course,' I smiled. This was the moment. He was going to offer me $1 million for *Tubular Bells* with a massive royalty. I could then accept and we could enjoy the rest of the night.

'I'd just like to make one thing clear. I don't care whether I sign Mike Oldfield or not,' he said, patting my arm. 'But I don't want any misunderstanding: both these girls are for me.'

Ahmet Ertegun eventually licensed *Tubular Bells* in the US and sold it as the music for a film. *The Exorcist* became a success in the States, and so did the album. It finally reached the top of the charts a year after it had done so in Britain.

Chapter 5   The next big thing 1974–1977

Every record company wants to make its bands famous so that people will buy its albums. When a band has a lot of admirers, it is quite easy to predict how many copies their next record will sell. Big names like Stevie Wonder and Paul McCartney sell worldwide. Promoting exports is difficult for any company, but music is one business that flies over most boundaries: it is carried by the radio and by word of mouth. It is also easier for an English-language song to sell around the world.

Simon and I developed three key aims when we negotiated with bands. First, we wanted to own copyright for as long as possible. Beneath all the excitement of dealing with musicians, the only value lay in the copyright of their songs. We also tried to include a musician's previous records in our contract, although often these were made by other record labels. We would offer high initial sums, but ask the artist to make their next eight albums with us. During the life of Virgin Music, we were proud that we never lost a band.

The second thing we always insisted on was including worldwide copyright to the musician's work in our contracts. Our last negotiating point was to make sure that Virgin owned the copyright in the individual members of the band as well as the band itself. Some bands broke up and the members became individually successful. Genesis is perhaps the best example, as Peter Gabriel and Phil Collins both became bigger stars outside Genesis than they had been within the band.

We also found that if we really wanted a band, we had to get them however much money we paid. Part of the secret of running a record label was to keep finding new bands and making them successful. Even if we lost money through a well-known band, it could help us to attract other musicians.

Using these principles, Virgin began to make contracts with new bands. Most of these would inevitably fail. We still paid ourselves tiny wages and we reinvested all the money we earned from *Tubular Bells* in building up the company.

♦

Kristen and I had been married for two years. We were having some difficulties. Kristen never had any peace from the constant stream of Virgin staff and bands who came in and out of the house every evening. Whenever I came home, the telephone would ring as soon as I shut the front door behind me. Wherever I am, I always pick up the phone. Other businessmen may say, 'I'll call you back,' but I've never been able to do that.

By 1974 our marriage was falling apart and we were both having affairs. Kristen wanted a more secure relationship. It is strange looking back on those years because I think that I loved Kristen more than she loved me. I wouldn't spend more than a night with another woman, but when Kristen started having affairs they turned into relationships. I remember driving her to the house of one man she was having an affair with, and begging her not to go inside. Then I went to pick her up the next morning and begged her not to go back.

One night we had dinner with Kevin Ayers and his wife. During the evening it became clear that Kevin liked Kristen and I liked Kevin's wife. We soon found ourselves chatting on two separate sofas, then kissing, and then Kevin and Kristen went off to his bedroom while his wife and I stayed on the sofa.

Something amazing happened between Kristen and Kevin that night. What started as harmless fun resulted in Kristen leaving me and moving in with Kevin. After a few weeks they started travelling around Europe. I tried to persuade her to come back to me, but she refused. She finally told me that we couldn't live together and I had to accept that I had lost her.

As well as my marriage breaking up in 1974, Virgin Music was beginning to have problems. It was in danger of being seen as just Mike Oldfield's label. Simon and I wanted new acts to balance Mike Oldfield's success. During the next few months, we tried and failed to sign up a number of bands including 10cc, The Who and Pink Floyd. It seemed that we were always the second choice.

By 1976 our catalogue was full of wonderful music, but we did not have enough really big acts. We were also short of cash. We had a crisis meeting with Simon, Nik and Ken Berry. Ken had started in the Notting Hill record shop as a clerk, but he soon had many other jobs. Whenever we needed to know anything, Ken knew all the answers. He was quiet but, as well as dealing with numbers, his great skill was dealing with people. He could negotiate with top musicians and their lawyers, and soon he became involved in contract negotiations. In many ways Ken became the link that held Nik, Simon and me together.

At the crisis meeting, we went through the figures of the shops, which were busy but not profitable. Then we started looking at the bands.

'It's clear to me,' Ken Berry said. 'We have to seriously consider getting rid of all our bands apart from Mike Oldfield.'

We looked at him in amazement.

'All our other bands are losing us money,' he went on. 'If we sacked at least half our staff, then we could cope, but at the moment Mike Oldfield is supporting the entire company.'

I have always believed that the only way to cope with a cash crisis is to try to expand out of it. 'What if we found ten more Mike Oldfields?' I asked. 'Would that be OK?'

We had two options: either put away some money and not take any more risks, or use our last few pounds to sign up another band that could succeed. If we chose the second, Virgin could lose everything within a few months, but at least we would have one last chance to succeed. From that night, we were desperately searching for The Next Big Thing.

♦

In the last week of November I was working in my office when I heard an extraordinary song being played in Simon's office. I ran downstairs to see him.

'What was that?' I asked.

'It's called "Anarchy in the UK". It's by The Sex Pistols.'

'Is it selling well?'

'Very well,' Simon admitted. 'Very well indeed.'

'Which company do they belong to?'

'EMI. I refused to give them a contract a couple of months ago. I could have made a mistake.'

There was something so powerful about the song that I was determined to see whether we could win them back. A few days later, I called the head of EMI but he was too busy to take my call. I left a message with his secretary saying that if he ever wanted to get rid of The Sex Pistols, then he should contact me. Half an hour later she called me back to say that EMI were quite happy with The Sex Pistols, thank you.

That same evening, The Sex Pistols were interviewed on an afternoon television show. The four musicians were drunk and used bad language. The next day the national press were angry at their bad behaviour. As I was reading an article about how someone had kicked their television in disgust at the show, the telephone rang. It was before 7 a.m. and it was the head of EMI.

'Please come and see me immediately,' he said. 'I hear that you are interested in The Sex Pistols.'

I went straight round to EMI's offices. Leslie Hill and I agreed that EMI would transfer The Sex Pistols to Virgin if Malcolm McLaren, the group's manager, agreed. We shook hands. Then Malcolm McLaren was brought in from the next room.

'Virgin have offered to take The Sex Pistols,' Hill said, trying unsuccessfully to keep the relief out of his voice.

'Excellent,' McLaren said, offering me his hand. 'I'll come to your offices later this afternoon.'

He never arrived and never returned my phone calls the next day. I stopped ringing him after four attempts. He knew how to reach me, but he didn't call.

On 9 March 1977, McLaren signed The Sex Pistols to A&M records. I sat at my desk and wondered about Malcolm McLaren. I knew that he had a bestseller on his hands. Virgin Music needed to change, and The Sex Pistols could do it for us.

A&M held a party to celebrate The Sex Pistols' contract. The Sex Pistols hated them; they hated all record companies – or at least they pretended to. After the signing, Sid Vicious, the lead singer, wrecked the office of Derek Green, the head of the company, and was sick all over his desk. When I heard this I reached for my telephone. To my delight, Derek Green told me he no longer wanted the band.

'Can we have them?' I asked.

'If you can cope with them,' he said. 'We certainly can't.'

The Sex Pistols were given £75,000 by A&M as compensation for the cancelled contract. Together with the £50,000 they had been given by EMI, they had earned £125,000 for doing nothing more than using bad language, being sick and one song. Once again, The Sex Pistols were looking for a record label.

Malcolm McLaren had done well. The Sex Pistols were now the most shocking band in the country. They had a single called 'God Save The Queen' which they wanted to release in time for the Queen's Silver Jubilee* Day in 1977.

I watched and waited. As Jubilee Day came closer, nobody else came forward to sign. I knew that Virgin records was perhaps the only record label that could do it. We had no shareholders to protest, no parent company or boss to tell me not to. On 12 May 1977 Malcolm McLaren finally came to see us. Virgin signed the British rights for The Sex Pistols' first album for £15,000, with another £50,000 for the rights for the rest of the world.

'Do you realize what you're getting into?' McLaren asked me.

'I do,' I assured him. 'The question is, do you?'

From the moment we signed, McLaren was looking for ways to make us get rid of them. To his horror we refused to be shocked. We released 'God Save The Queen', which was banned by BBC radio and rose to number two in the charts. The Sex Pistols made Virgin famous again as a record company that could create a huge amount of publicity.

* Silver Jubilee: a celebration of twenty-five years as Queen.

Chapter 6   Living on the edge 1976–1980

One weekend in early 1976 I met my future wife, Joan Templeman, at the Manor. I make my mind up about someone within thirty seconds of meeting them, and I fell in love with Joan from the moment I saw her. The problem was that she was already married to someone else, a record producer and musician who was producing a Virgin band called Wigwam.

Joan was a sensible Scots lady. She had been married to Ronnie Leahy for almost eight years, but they had no children. Ronnie travelled a lot, and it seemed to me that he and Joan had begun to move apart. Whenever Ronnie was away, I called Joan's friends and asked whether they were seeing Joan.

'Mind if I come along?' I asked.

It was unlike the other affairs I'd had, which I'd been able to control. Joan is a very private person, and I had very little idea what she thought of me.

Eventually Joan agreed to come with me to the Isle of Wight* and we spent the weekend in a tiny hotel. Our affair continued for almost a year. We knew that we were in danger of causing pain to Ronnie. In some ways Joan and Ronnie had a similar relationship to Kristen's and mine: Ronnie had wanted to experiment with sleeping with other women, and had told Joan that she needed to have broader experiences too. Joan didn't want a series of short relationships, and so she gradually began to fall in love with me.

Our affair became more complicated when Kristen heard that I was in love with Joan and arrived back in London. She told me that she wanted to get back together with me. My family has always believed that you work at your marriage, and so I felt I had to agree. But I was in love with Joan. It was an awful

* Isle of Wight: an island off the south coast of England.

situation for each of us: Joan felt torn between me and Ronnie; Kristen had been torn between me and Kevin; and I now felt torn between Kristen and Joan. What had started off as a dream affair was beginning to destroy five people's lives.

I was at a party with both Joan and Kristen. Joan's best friend Linda found me: 'So who are you actually in love with?' she demanded. 'This can't go on. You're all killing yourselves and you need to sort it out.'

I saw Joan talking to someone else.

'I'm in love with one woman,' I said, looking across at Joan. 'But she's not in love with me.'

'I'm telling you that she is,' said Linda, following my look.

The next night I was alone. It was a dark February night and raining hard. I was on the telephone so I didn't hear the sound of knocking. Then the door opened and I swung round. It was Joan.

'I'll call you back later,' I said to the phone.

'Well, I thought I'd move in,' Joan said.

◆

I like to get away from London in the middle of winter. I've found that sunshine and long-distance travel give me a clearer view of London life. This time I had two extra reasons to get away from the city: I wanted to take Johnny Rotten with me to Jamaica because he was having some difficulties with The Sex Pistols and Malcolm McLaren. I also hoped to meet Joan, who was going to Los Angeles with Ronnie to give their marriage one last chance. Johnny Rotten was delighted to come because he loved West Indian music, and Joan and I agreed not to speak until she had decided on her future.

At the last minute Simon was unable to come, so I went with Ken. We stayed at the Kingston Sheraton and a stream of bands started coming round to our room.

We signed almost twenty bands in a week. I tried to persuade Johnny to stay with The Sex Pistols, but it didn't work. He told me that the group were arguing among themselves and with Malcolm McLaren; that Sid Vicious was taking all kinds of drugs and growing violent with Nancy, his girlfriend. Johnny wanted to form a new band called PiL, Public Image Limited. Although I kept turning the conversation back to what The Sex Pistols could do, Johnny was not really listening.

I had to accept that Virgin would never make much money from The Sex Pistols. Although it was upsetting to see them fall apart, at least Virgin had now become a smart record label. New, exciting bands were approaching us. Virgin Music Publishing had signed a schoolteacher from Newcastle called Gordon Sumner who used the stage name 'Sting'.

Joan left a message at the hotel asking me to call her. 'Shall we meet in New York?' she asked.

I left Jamaica the next morning.

Her attempt to save her marriage had failed. We spent a week in Manhattan and felt like refugees. My divorce from Kristen had not yet been finalized, and Joan had only just separated from Ronnie. We were thinking of escaping from New York to spend some time together alone away from the telephone, when somebody asked me if I had named Virgin Music after the Virgin Islands. The answer was no – but it sounded like just the place that Joan and I needed.

We decided to fly down to the Virgin Islands. We had nowhere to stay and not much money, but I heard that if you appeared seriously interested in buying an island the local salesman would let you stay in a grand house and fly you around by helicopter. This sounded rather fun. I made a few calls. I introduced myself and mentioned that Virgin Music was expanding and we wanted to buy an island where our rock stars could come and escape. The salesman began to get very excited.

The next day we were flown all over the Virgin Islands and shown the islands that were for sale. 'There's one more which is a real jewel,' he said. 'It's called Necker Island, but it's in the middle of nowhere.'

'All right,' I said. 'Please can we see it?'

We landed on a white sandy beach. 'It's the most beautiful island in the Virgin Islands,' said the salesman, 'but it needs a lot of money spent on it.'

'How much is it?' I asked.

'£3 million.'

Our visions of watching the sunset from the island faded.

'How much were you thinking of spending?' the salesman asked suspiciously.

'We could offer £150,000,' I said brightly. '$200,000,' I added, trying to make it sound more.

'I see.'

As we flew back, it was clear that we were no longer welcome. Our bags were left at the door, and Joan and I took them across to a small hotel. But we were determined to buy Necker. We felt that it could be somewhere we could always escape to. We promised to return.

Back in London, I found out that the owner of Necker Island wanted to sell in a hurry. He wanted to build somewhere in Scotland for around £200,000. I increased my offer to £175,000 and waited for three months. Finally I got a call.

'If you offer £180,000, it's yours.'

I agreed immediately. Even at such a low price, there was a problem: the Virgin Islands government said that whoever bought Necker Island would have to develop it within five years or its ownership would pass to them. It would cost a lot to build a house and pipe water across from the neighbouring island, but I was determined to make enough money to afford it.

Joan and I stayed on Beef Island for the rest of that holiday, and there I set up Virgin Airways. We were trying to get to Puerto Rico, but the local flight was cancelled. The airport was full of passengers. I made a few calls, and rented a plane for $2,000. I divided the price by the number of seats, borrowed a blackboard, and wrote VIRGIN AIRWAYS: $39 SINGLE FLIGHT TO PUERTO RICO. I walked around the airport and soon filled every seat on the plane. As we landed, a passenger turned to me and said: 'Virgin Airways isn't too bad – smarten up the service a little and you could be in business.'

'I might just do that,' I laughed.

◆

In 1977 Virgin made a pre-tax profit of £400,000; in 1978 the figure increased to £500,000. After the break-up of The Sex Pistols, we were left with a handful of our original artists. The most important was Mike Oldfield, whose albums still sold well. We also had a couple of new bands: Orchestral Manoeuvres in the Dark and The Human League.

By 1979, an outsider might have looked at Virgin and thought it was a collection of different companies. From our tiny house in Vernon Yard we operated the record shops, which Nik ran; the record company, which was run by Simon and Ken; and the music publishing company, which was run by Carol Wilson. The Manor was going well, and we had expanded our recording business by purchasing a London recording studio. The original plan to set up everything that a musician needed – recording, publishing, distribution and retailing – was beginning to work. We also started Virgin Book Publishing, which published books about music and autobiographies of musicians.

Nik had also set up The Venue, a nightclub where our bands could play. It was clear that bands no longer wanted simply to record their songs and then release them. Pop videos were becoming the most effective way to promote songs, so Nik set up a film studio where our bands could make their own videos.

The other service that Virgin should offer our artists was to sell their records abroad. The best measure of a group's success is how many records it sells overseas. The large companies had a huge advantage over Virgin since they had representatives in France and Germany.

One option was for Virgin to concentrate on the domestic market and license bands overseas in the same way that we had licensed Mike Oldfield. Although this was a cheap option, it limited growth. When you license a band to another record company, you lose control of their promotion. We wanted to control our British bands overseas, and we also wanted to attract overseas bands to Virgin. We wanted French, German and American bands to sign with us for worldwide rights.

With a small staff it was difficult to imagine that we could rival the large record companies, but we decided to try. In 1978, Ken went to New York to set up the Virgin label in America.

In 1979 I went to France to meet Jacques Kerner, the French head of PolyGram. Although I was supposed to be seeing him to ask PolyGram to distribute Virgin records, I was really looking for somebody who could set up Virgin in France. Kerner introduced me to Patrick Zelnick, who ran PolyGram's record side.

After the meeting I thanked both men and asked them to call and see me when they were next in London. The next month Patrick called me. We had lunch and I asked him whether he would leave PolyGram and set up Virgin in France. I would give him complete independence to sign any bands he liked. We worked out some figures and Patrick agreed to do it.

'When you're invited for dinner,' Jacques Kerner said to me in a phone call when Patrick resigned, 'you shouldn't walk away with the knives and forks.'

I apologized, but told Jacques that Patrick had made his own decision. One of the first bands he contracted was called

Telephone; they became the bestselling band of the year in France. Years later, Patrick would shake his head in disbelief that he had left the security of PolyGram and joined an almost bankrupt English record company.

I went back to France to meet the managing director of Arista Records. We were unable to agree a distribution deal, but I was interested when he started talking about how Arista was going to contract Julien Clerc. I had no idea who Julien Clerc was. I excused myself, went to the bathroom, wrote 'Julien Claire' on my wrist and then carefully pulled down the sleeve of my sweater to hide it. After the meeting, I rushed to a call box and telephoned Patrick.

'Have you heard of a singer called Julien Claire?' I asked.

'Of course,' Patrick said. 'He's the biggest star in France.'

'Well, he's free to sign a contract. Can we meet him for lunch tomorrow?'

Patrick and I persuaded Julien Clerc to sign with Virgin. Within a fortnight I had upset two record companies, but both Julien Clerc and Patrick made a lot of money for Virgin France and themselves.

Virgin was growing into a large company. We had very good sales, and were making as much money as any regular business. But the bankers never saw it like that. 'You're doing very well,' the bank manager said. 'But the quality of your earnings is poor. We can't see what they're going to be more than a month in advance.'

Despite this analysis, at the end of 1978 we felt confident: in the UK we had enjoyed a good year, with a number of successes and good sales through the record shops. But in 1979 Margaret Thatcher was elected head of the British government; interest rates went up, and the economy suffered. Record sales in Britain dropped for the first time in twenty years, and our shops lost a lot of money. Ken had no luck in New York: Virgin's first single there cost $50,000 to promote and failed. We decided to close the office, and called Ken back home.

Nik estimated that Virgin would make a £1 million loss in 1980. We were suddenly in serious trouble. For the second time we had to make some staff redundant: nine people, a sixth of the worldwide staff of Virgin Music. Nik, Simon, Ken and I spent hours arguing over what we should do. Once again we went through our catalogue of bands and made several cuts.

Nik and Simon argued about which bands Virgin should keep. Nik argued that Virgin should drop The Human League, a young band from Sheffield.

'Over my dead body,' Simon told him.

'But we can't afford to keep supporting them,' Nik said.

'The Human League is exactly why I'm in this business,' Simon said, fighting to keep his temper.

'You spend all the money I save on the shops,' Nik said.

I watched them fight, knowing that I had to do something. Nik was my main partner, my closest childhood friend, and we had worked together since we were sixteen. But he was determined to cut back and save money. I felt that unless we spent money, we would never get out of trouble.

I supported Simon; I felt that Simon's taste in music was the only thing that could help Virgin survive.

At another meeting we argued about the drummer from Genesis. Simon wanted to spend £65,000 on a contract with Phil Collins. We knew it was a risk. Nik finally agreed that we should sign Phil Collins, and even took money from the shop tills for the advance payment. Phil was a brilliant musician and singer and became more successful than Genesis itself.

A couple of months later, I found two very attractive deals. They both involved nightclubs – The Roof Garden and Heaven. Heaven was a large gay nightclub. The owner was a friend of my sister Vanessa and he wanted to sell it to someone who would respect it and keep it as a gay club. Through my work at the Advisory Centre, he knew that he could trust me to do this.

I knew that Nik would oppose these purchases, so I signed the contracts without telling him. He was very angry. He thought I was leading Virgin into bankruptcy, and wanted to protect his 40 per cent share of the business. I had been unhappy with our professional relationship for two or three years. I felt that Nik was always trying to stop me risking money on new bands. We both realized that it was best to separate while we were still friends.

I raised a loan from another bank and bought Nik's share in Virgin. As well as this cash, Nik also took some of his favourite parts of the Virgin group, including the film and video studios. He later made wonderful films, including the prize-winning *The Crying Game*.

Chapter 7 'Nobody will get on a plane called "Virgin".' 1980–1984

As well as parting from Nik, I came dangerously close to losing Joan in 1980. I was working hard to keep Virgin going. However late I got home, the telephone rang. Every time we woke up on a Saturday morning, it rang again. One night I returned home and found Joan had gone. She had left me a note: 'I am pregnant. I am afraid to tell you. I have run away from home. If you miss me, call me at Rose's.'

I sat there holding Joan's note and thinking about our unborn baby, and I realized that I really loved her. I called Rose, Joan's sister, and rushed round to be with Joan.

After about six months of pregnancy, Joan was taken ill and had to have an operation. This started the birth. We were in Scotland at the time and set off immediately to reach a more modern hospital at Inverness. The drive across Scotland in the snow was frightening. By the time we arrived, she was in great pain and was desperately trying to keep the baby inside her.

It became clear that Joan would have to give birth to the baby. There was little chance of the baby surviving as it was three months early. A baby girl was born who weighed less than two kilograms, and we called her Clare after my aunt. She could scarcely take food, and the hospital did not have the equipment to keep her alive.

Although Clare did open her lovely, deep blue eyes, she died after four days. All I can remember of her now is her size. Neither of us was allowed to hold or touch her. She was so small and lived for so little time, but she brought Joan and me close together. We were determined to have another baby, and to our delight Joan became pregnant again within a year.

Once again the baby was early, this time by six weeks. Holly was born under three kilograms in weight. It was the most amazing experience. I promised myself that I would never miss the birth of one of our children.

♦

In 1981 Virgin Music finally began to earn some money. Whenever Virgin has money, I always search for new opportunities. I am continually trying to broaden the Group so we do not depend on a narrow source of income. This time I saw the perfect opportunity.

Londoners traditionally read a magazine called *Time Out* to find out what's going on in the city. I had spoken to the owner of *Time Out*, Tony Elliott, a number of times about buying the magazine. In the spring of 1981, he had an argument with his staff and they walked out. I thought we could seize the opportunity and publish our own magazine, *Event*.

Knowing that *Event* was planned, Tony Elliott rapidly got his staff back to work. Some of the more political staff broke away from *Time Out* and formed their own magazine, *City Limits*.

The new *Time Out* was published on 18 September. The following week the first *City Limits* came out, together with our magazine *Event*. There were too many magazines on the London market and Virgin did not have the cash to support a new project. When *Event* failed to sell many copies, I decided to close it down.

It is always difficult to admit failure, but I also learnt a lesson. I realized that it was important to separate the various Virgin companies so that if one failed, it would not threaten the rest of the Virgin Group. Every successful businessman sometimes fails, and many have faced bankruptcy. We paid our debts and shut down the magazine.

The money that *Event* magazine lost Virgin was rapidly repaid by The Human League, Simple Minds, Phil Collins' successful album *Face Value*, and a young singer called Boy George.

From the £900,000 loss in 1980, we made a profit of £2 million in 1982. In 1983 our profits rose to £11 million.

♦

Soon after Nik left, two things happened that could not have been predicted. Firstly, CDs became popular so we were able to resell previously released records on CD. The second change was that Virgin became the leading independent record label. Virgin Music began to dominate the top-ten singles and album charts.

As I watched the money pouring into the bank, I began to think of other ways to use it. I needed another challenge. I thought about expanding our tiny book-publishing business. I thought that if a musician is famous, they could explore different activities, including books and videos and appearances in films.

My sister Vanessa suggested I talked to her boyfriend, Robert Devereux, who worked for Macmillan Publishers. Robert thought that books and videos could be sold in the same shops, and that Virgin Books could involve television, radio, films and videos as well as books. Although we were still a tiny publishing company, Robert left his job and came to join us.

He made Virgin Books a specialist publisher of books about music and sport. A few years later he bought another publishing house, WH Allen, which he put together with Virgin Books. This was a mistake: we tried to do too much and in 1989 the publishing business ran into difficulties. It was one of our early purchases, and we learnt how painful it was to make staff redundant. It also illustrated the benefits of starting a company from nothing, when you can employ the people you want.

A year later Rob Shreeve, Robert's boss from Macmillan, joined Virgin. Together they changed the business into Virgin Publishing. Within a few years the company had become highly successful, and probably the world's leading publisher of books on popular music.

As Virgin Music grew, Robert wanted more money to invest in what we called Virgin Vision. He wanted Virgin Vision to be involved in the British film industry. Rather than making films, Robert began to push Virgin into distributing videos and films instead. He started distributing pop videos for all record companies. He also bought previously released old movies and distributed them as videos. Virgin Video grew into a large distributor of films and videos with sales passing £50 million by the late 1980s.

A number of people suggested ideas that would have increased Virgin's role in entertainment, but my imagination was caught by another proposal. In February 1984 a young American lawyer called Randolph Fields asked me whether I was interested in operating an airline.

◆

Randolph Fields wanted investors for a new airline that would use the London Gatwick to New York route, which had become vacant after the failure of Sir Freddie Laker's airline in 1982.

I make up my mind about a business proposal within about thirty seconds of looking at it. I rely more on instinct than on numbers. This might be because, due to my dyslexia, I distrust numbers, which I feel can be twisted to prove anything. The idea of operating a Virgin airline grabbed my imagination, but I had to work out what the risks were.

The only airline that was offering cheap flights across the Atlantic in 1984 was People Express. I picked up the phone and tried to call them. Their number was busy and it was impossible to get through all morning. Either People Express was very poorly managed and therefore they were an easy target for new competition, or they were so busy that there was room for new competition.

I called Simon on Sunday evening. 'What do you think about starting an airline?' I asked him. 'I've got a proposal here –'

'For God's sake!' he interrupted me. 'You're crazy.'

'I'm serious.'

On Monday morning I found the number for Boeing in Seattle and called them. They were rather confused to hear an Englishman asking them what kinds of deals were available on a jet plane. I spent all afternoon and evening talking to Boeing, and eventually I spoke to somebody who could help me. They told me that Boeing did rent out aircraft, and that they had a second-hand jet that they would take back after a year if things didn't work. With this information, I faced Simon and Ken. The meeting was not a success.

'You're crazy, Richard,' Simon said. 'We've been friends for years, but if you do this I'm not sure that we can carry on working together.'

Ken also thought that the idea of combining a record company with an airline was not good. 'I can't see the connection,' he said.

'All right, then,' I said. 'We'll keep the two companies separate.

46

We'll arrange the finance so that Virgin Music is not at risk. I've spoken to Boeing and they say that they will take the plane back after a year if it doesn't work. The most Virgin would lose would be £2 million.' Simon and Ken remained opposed.

In the same way that the argument over The Human League had changed my relationship with Nik, this argument altered my relationship with Simon. He felt that I was prepared to bet the company on a crazy scheme. Simon's interests and love for life come from music, books, paintings and beautiful cars. My interest in life comes from setting myself challenges and trying to rise above them. Commercially, Simon was right, but I felt I had to attempt it. After that lunchtime our relationship became increasingly tense.

Randolph wanted to call the airline British Atlantic, but I wanted to bring 'Virgin' into the title. There was a lot to learn, so I asked Sir Freddie Laker, a man I have always admired, whether he could help me. Two of the best ideas that came out of our lunch together were to offer cars to pick up passengers and to offer a free economy ticket to anyone who flew business class. Freddie also warned me to expect some fierce competition from British Airways.

'They're very tough,' he said. 'My mistake was that I never complained loudly enough. They destroyed my financing and it's too late for me now. I took them to court and won millions of dollars, but I lost my airline. If you ever get into trouble, sue them before it's too late.'

◆

The first arrangement I made with Randolph was that we would be equal partners. I would invest the money; he would run the airline. He had already found two key people: Roy Gardener, who had run the engineering side of Laker Airways, and David Tait, who had run the American side of the operation.

'What do you think of the name British Atlantic?' I asked David Tait.

'Just what the world needs: another BA,' he said.

Using David's reaction, I managed to get Randolph to agree to change the name to Virgin Atlantic Airways.

'What do you think of the new name?' I asked David Tait.

'Virgin Atlantic? Nobody will ever get on a plane called "Virgin". It's ridiculous.'

Within a couple of weeks it was clear that the arrangement between Randolph and me would not work. At our first meeting in front of the Civil Aviation Authority, who check the safety of planes, Randolph went in to talk about his plans for the new airline. He was fiercely questioned by representatives of another airline, British Caledonian, who were objecting to us. Randolph was an impatient man and he grew angry and confused. When the CAA questioned our finances, the British Caledonian lawyer looked at me and said, 'You'll have to have a lot of successful records to support an airline.'

'Actually,' I pointed out, 'Virgin made profits of £11 million last year – more than twice those of your client.'

The CAA said that the new airline would have to have capital of £3 million, and gave their permission for us to fly. Of course, they could withdraw their permission at any time if we failed to meet safety requirements.

We rented space near Gatwick Airport, where we based Roy Gardner and his engineering team, and we started looking for pilots and air crew.

The first major problem was my relationship with Randolph Fields. Two things became clear. Since the Virgin Group was guaranteeing the finances of Virgin Atlantic, our bank would not lend us money if we controlled only half the new airline. Since Randolph was not supplying any money, he was forced to agree that Virgin should have a controlling share of the airline.

A more difficult problem with Randolph was his relationship with the new Virgin Atlantic staff. I first realized there was serious trouble from David Tait.

'I've resigned,' he told me. 'I'm sorry, but Randolph is impossible to work with.' I knew that without David selling tickets in the US, Virgin Atlantic would be in serious trouble. I begged him to come and see me in London. He had no money to buy a ticket, so I sent him one and he came two days later.

David's argument with Randolph was about the ticket system. Randolph wanted to avoid all travel agents, who charged 10 per cent of the fare for their services, and to sell every ticket through a company called Ticketron that sold theatre tickets. David argued that since the 30,000 travel agents across America sell 90 per cent of all airline tickets, we needed to use them. Also, Ticketron only had six New York offices, which was not enough to sell 200 tickets for each flight to the UK. David had finally come to an agreement with an airline ticketing system owned by the American businessman and politician Ross Perot. When Randolph heard about this he was very angry and shouted down the telephone at David. David decided that he didn't need to be shouted at by a 29-year-old lawyer who didn't know how the airline industry worked.

The staff also complained about Randolph's behaviour. I realized that Randolph was not the person to run a new airline. I promised David that if he stayed he would have no more trouble from Randolph. 'He won't be here much longer,' I said. 'You can deal with me directly.'

As we worked through April and May, Randolph was cut out of the operation. He became increasingly difficult to deal with. Eventually my lawyers advised me to change the locks on the ticketing office to keep him out. As the first flight in June came nearer, Randolph and I were at war.

Chapter 8   Taking the Virgin Group public
1984–1988

On 19 June 1984, three days before we were due to start our flights, I went down to Gatwick for a test flight which would give us final CAA approval. The entire flight crew and over a hundred Virgin staff came as well, and I sat at the back with the CAA official. We took off and the crew clapped and cheered. I wanted to cry because I felt so proud of everyone.

Then there was a loud bang from outside and a massive flash of flame, and black smoke poured out from one of the engines.

In that horrible silence, the CAA official put his arm around my shoulders. 'Don't worry, Richard,' he said. 'These things happen.'

Some birds had been sucked into an engine, which exploded. We needed a new engine overnight to do the CAA test flight again.

Unfortunately, because Virgin Atlantic did not have a CAA licence, we were not insured for the engine. We had to pay £600,000 for a new one. I called our bank to let them know that a payment of £600,000 would have to go through our account.

'You're very close to your limit,' Chris Rashbrook, the manager of our Coutts account said. Our overdraft with the bank for the entire Virgin Group was set at £3 million.

'Please can you wait until I get this flight finished?' I asked. 'Let's sort it out when I get home.' He said he'd think about it.

The day before the flight, the plane was fitted with another engine and ready to fly again. This time it did not explode and we were given our licence. I hurried back to London to sort out another Randolph Fields crisis. We had offered Randolph £1 million, but he thought that wasn't enough. He had gone to a judge in the US and asked him to stop our plane from taking off. All through the night we had meetings with David Tait, Roy

Gardner and my lawyers to stop Randolph ruining the airline. The judge eventually dismissed the request.

During that first flight I was surrounded by family and friends, the people who had been most important to me and to Virgin over the last ten years.

I took the return flight back to Gatwick and fell into my first long sleep for many weeks. When I woke up, I felt sure that nothing else could go wrong. A bad mistake.

A taxi carried me back to London. As we stopped outside my house, I saw a rather uncomfortable-looking man sitting on the steps. It was Chris Rashbrook. I invited him in. He told me that Coutts could not extend Virgin's overdraft and would refuse any cheques that took our overdraft over £3 million. I rarely lose my temper, but if this bank manager refused our cheques, Virgin would be out of business within days. Nobody would supply an airline with fuel or food if people heard that our cheques were no good.

'Excuse me,' I said. 'You are not welcome in my house. Please get out.' I took him by the arm and led him to the front door and pushed him outside. Then I had a shower and called Ken.

'We've got to get as much money in from overseas as possible today. And then we've got to find new bankers.'

We managed to pull in enough money from overseas to keep us below the £3 million overdraft limit. The Coutts crisis made me realize that we needed somebody tough to manage our finances, somebody who could cope with the finances of both Virgin Atlantic and Virgin Music and act as a bridge between the two.

The mid-1980s were good years in the City and every company seemed able to sell its shares to the public and raise millions of pounds to invest. I began to think that this was the way forward for Virgin.

Apart from the four main operations, Virgin Music, Virgin

Records shops, Virgin Vision and the new airline, there were now a lot of small companies operating under the Virgin name. These businesses needed someone to put them in order.

Don Cruickshank had been general manager of the *Sunday Times* and managing director of the *Financial Times*. With Don as managing director, Virgin began to be organized into a company that could attract outside investors. Soon he brought in Trevor Abbott as finance director. They held meetings with banks and rearranged our finances. The first thing they did was sort out our overdraft. Virgin was going to make more than £100 million in 1984. They went to a group of banks and arranged an overdraft of £30 million. They then looked at the Virgin Group and decided to close down a number of our smaller companies. They divided the Virgin Group into Music, Retail and Vision, and then moved Virgin Atlantic, together with Virgin Holidays, Heaven, The Roof Garden and Necker Island into a separate company. Simon and I were both thirty-three years old, as were Trevor and Ken. Don was a little older. We felt powerful, and we now decided to take the Virgin Group public. We were going into the stock market.

◆

I am often asked why I accept challenges with either powerboats or hot-air balloons. People say that with success, money and a happy family, I should stop taking risks. This is obviously true and part of me agrees with them. I love life; I love my family; and I am frightened by the idea of being killed and leaving Joan without a husband, and Holly and Sam without a father. But another part of me is driven to try new adventures. I want to experience as much as I can of life.

The first challenge I was involved in was to try and recapture the Blue Riband prize for Britain. This was given to the fastest boat that crossed the Atlantic.

In 1984, a powerboat builder called Ted Toleman asked me to

sponsor his boat and join him in the challenge. I was attracted by the idea of winning a prize for Britain, and I wanted to promote the new airline. A successful Atlantic crossing would attract publicity in both New York and London.

'How fit are you?' Chay Blyth, the round-the-world sailor and third member of our crew, asked me.

'Not bad,' I said.

'That's not good enough.'

I started the hardest training programme of my life.

We asked Esso to sponsor the trip by providing fuel and they kindly agreed to do so. We went along to a celebration lunch with their directors.

'I want to thank you,' I said. 'It's going to be a great trip and we're going to advertise BP as much as we can. We're going to put BP's name all over the fuel ships. Nobody will ever confuse you with that old rival of yours . . .'

At this point I looked at the wall opposite and noticed the huge Esso sign. I realized my mistake. The Esso executives looked at me with horror. I fell down on the floor and crawled under the table. Remarkably, Esso did not withdraw its sponsorship.

Joan was nearly eight months pregnant with our second child, and I was hoping to be back in time for the birth. But we were stuck in New York for three weeks waiting for stormy weather to clear. I kept flying back to London to be with Joan, then flying back to New York. I crossed the Atlantic eight times.

The storms cleared. Joan told me that she was OK and that I should go. There were still two weeks until the baby was due. Towards the end of the first day of the crossing, I got a radio message. 'Joan's in hospital and she's just had a baby boy. It all went fine.' I'd broken my promise to be present at the birth of my children, but most importantly we'd had a healthy child.

We went through three hellish days. As we approached Ireland with only a few hundred kilometres to go, we hit a fierce storm.

When we were less than a hundred kilometres from the Scilly Isles★ and the prize was almost in our hands, we hit a massive wave. A second later, our engineer shouted, 'We're going down! Get out fast.'

'Stay calm!' Chay shouted. 'There's no hurry! Everyone take their time.'

As we moved carefully towards the lifeboat, Chay shouted, 'We're going down! Get out!'

The lifeboat was tiny and we sat there waiting to be rescued. Ted was upset, his dream destroyed. We saw the end of our boat, the Virgin Challenger, sticking out above the water. The rest of the boat was underwater. All you could see was the word 'Virgin'.

'Well, Richard,' Chay said, pointing at the name. 'As usual, you've had the last word.'

Winning the Blue Riband was unfinished business. We formed a new team and on 15 May 1986, Virgin Atlantic Challenger II was revealed. We shipped it over to New York and waited for good weather. The trip up the east coast of the US was much faster than we hoped. After our second refuelling, the trouble started. The engines stopped and our engineer told us the fuel pipes were full of water. We had to empty the fuel tanks and refuel again, which took three hours. It was now 11 p.m. and a storm was coming in. We were soaked to the skin, very sick and our hair was frozen.

'It's not worth going on,' Chay shouted in my ear. 'It's over. I'm sorry, Richard.'

I knew that if we failed on this attempt there would be no third time. I had to persuade my companions to continue. 'Let's just see how far we can get. We've got to try,' I said.

There was an engine specialist on board the Esso refuelling

★ Scilly Isles: islands off the south-west coast of England.

boat and he came onto the boat to help us. There was still water in the fuel but we could empty it out as we moved.

'We can go on,' I said to Chay.

'It's over, Richard,' Chay shouted at me. 'This boat's finished.'

We stood there, angrily. Our eyes were red from the salt and the petrol smell and our hands were raw and bleeding. We hated this boat; we hated this trip; we hated the sea; we hated the weather; and at that moment, we hated each other.

'God, you're worse than me,' Chay said. 'All right, we'll try.'

When we passed the point where we had sunk on the previous attempt, we suddenly knew that we could do it. Eight kilometres from the Scilly Isles, we were met by helicopters and hundreds of small boats which welcomed us home. Our total journey lasted 3 days, 8 hours and 31 minutes; we had beaten the Blue Riband record by 2 hours and 9 minutes.

♦

I will never forget going into the City to see lines of people queuing up to buy Virgin shares – 70,000 people had already applied by post, but these people had left it until the last day, 13 November 1986. I walked up and down the queue thanking them, and some of their replies stuck in my mind.

'We're not going on holiday this year; we're putting our money into Virgin.'

'We're relying on you, Richard.'

More than 100,000 people wanted our shares and the Post Office brought in twenty extra staff to cope with the mail. Beneath our excitement, we were worried to hear that only a small number of City companies had applied for shares. It was the first sign of the difficulty we were going to have with the City.

By 1986 Virgin had become one of Britain's largest private companies, with about 4,000 employees. For the year ending in July 1986, Virgin had sales of £189 million compared with

£119 million for the previous year, an increase of around 60 per cent. Although we were a large company, we could not expand: all we could do was either use the cash we earned or ask our bankers for a bigger overdraft.

Selling shares to the public enabled Virgin to raise money which we could invest in new businesses; it would give us more freedom from the banks and make us more famous; and it would enable us to bid for Thorn EMI, the largest record label in the country. Don was enthusiastic about Virgin going public. Trevor and Ken were not keen, and warned me that we would all hate giving up our independence. I pushed away their negative arguments.

After the sale of shares, I owned 55 per cent of the Virgin Group; Simon owned 9 per cent; Ken, Don, Trevor and Robert and some of the other members of the staff had 2 per cent; the outside investors had 34 per cent. We had sold each Virgin share at 140 pence, and the Virgin Group was valued at £240 million. Of course this was only part of the company – Virgin Atlantic, Virgin Holidays and the nightclubs were all separate because the City felt that they were too financially risky to be part of the sale.

My life was as busy as ever. The mid-1980s and the start of Virgin Atlantic was the period when I started to use myself to promote Virgin. I found that the press enjoyed writing stories about Virgin if they could put a face to the name. And so my name and the Virgin brand name became one.

◆

Although we had raised £30 million from the sale of shares, I soon began to feel that we had made the wrong decision. The City made heavy demands on us and I found it difficult to cope with all the formality the City insisted we adopt. I was used to chatting to Simon and Ken about which bands to sign contracts with, and then letting them get on with it. Virgin board meetings had always been very informal affairs.

I also had a number of disagreements with Don about dividends. I didn't want to follow British tradition and pay out a large dividend. I preferred the American or Japanese tradition where a company reinvests its profits to build itself and increase the value of its shares.

These arguments illustrated the general loss of control I experienced. Previously I was confident about any decisions we made, but now I was less confident and wondered whether every decision should be formally agreed at a board meeting. In many ways, 1987 was Virgin's least creative year. We spent at least 50 per cent of our time going to the City to explain what we were doing instead of just doing it.

Virgin shares, which had started trading at 140 pence, soon fell to 120 pence. The faith which people had placed in me by spending their own money on buying Virgin shares began to frighten me.

As 1987 progressed, the Virgin share price recovered to around 140 pence, but it never went much higher. We began to use the money we had raised to make two investments. The first was to set up Virgin in the US; the second was to take over Thorn EMI. We felt that the EMI record label was managed in rather a sleepy way and that their catalogue, which included The Beatles, could be run much more profitably. The Thorn EMI Group was valued at around £750 million. I thought that the best thing to do was go round and have a chat with Sir Colin Southgate, the managing director of Thorn EMI, and ask him in a friendly way whether he would like to sell us EMI Music.

I called Sir Colin and arranged a meeting at his office. I went alone. I was taken into a room where I was faced by at least twenty unsmiling faces. Sir Colin shook my hand and looked over my shoulder to see whether there was anyone else. I sat down and looked across at the faces.

'Well, let me introduce you,' Sir Colin began. He gave me

the names of bankers, lawyers and management consultants.

'I'm Richard Branson,' I introduced myself with a nervous laugh. 'I just wondered whether you would like to . . . like to sell EMI Music. It seems to me that Thorn EMI is such a big group that EMI Music might not be your top priority.'

There was a long silence.

'We're quite happy with EMI,' Sir Colin said.

'Oh, well,' I said. 'It was worth a try.' I stood up and left the room. I went straight round to see Simon and Ken.

'If Sir Colin's so worried that he brought those people along, then they are clearly in trouble,' I said. 'I think we should bid for them.' Simon and Ken agreed with me.

We knew that our first year's profits as a public company were going to be over £30 million, so we planned to announce this in October. At the same time we would announce our bid for Thorn EMI. During the summer, we arranged a £100 million loan with the Bank of Nova Scotia and slowly began buying shares in Thorn EMI. Through the summer months there were some rumours that Thorn EMI was in trouble, and I began to worry that October might be too late for our bid. There was not much I could do about it, because I was setting off on a challenge which many people thought would kill me. Per Lindstrand and I were planning to fly across the Atlantic Ocean in a hot-air balloon.

◆

Per Lindstrand had phoned me with his proposal. 'I'm planning to build the world's largest hot-air balloon, and fly it at 9,000 metres. I believe that it can cross the Atlantic.'

I knew that Per Lindstrand was a world expert at ballooning. He explained that nobody had flown a hot-air balloon further than 960 kilometres. To cross the Atlantic, we would have to fly 4,800 kilometres.

I asked Per to come and see me. 'I'll never understand the

science and the theory,' I said, 'but I'll come with you if you answer one question.'

'Of course.' Per stiffened his back, ready for a challenging question.

'Do you have any children?'

'Yes, I have two.'

'OK, then.' I stood up and shook his hand. 'I'll come. But I'd better learn how to fly one of these things first.'

Per took me for a week's course on ballooning in Spain. It was one of the most exciting things I had ever done. I was ready — and I was scared.

◆

After ten hours we had flown 1,440 kilometres from Maine in the US, and easily broken the long-distance record for a hot-air balloon. After twenty-nine hours, we crossed the coast of Ireland. The speed of our journey gave us an unexpected problem: we still had three full tanks of fuel that could explode when we landed. We decided to go very low and drop the fuel tanks in an empty field before we came down for a controlled landing. Suddenly the wind blew us harder than we expected, we hit the ground and the fuel tanks were torn off. Without their weight, we flew back upwards. We were completely out of control and the wind swept us out to sea.

We came down again, this time into the Irish Sea.

'Get out!' Per shouted at me. 'Richard, we've got to get out.' He threw himself into the cold black water. I waited for a moment, then I realized that it was too late. Without Per's weight, the huge balloon moved quickly upwards. I went up into thick cloud and lost sight of everything. I was by myself, flying the biggest balloon ever built and moving towards Scotland.

Whatever I did in the next ten minutes would lead to my death or survival. Per was either dead or trying to swim. I had to get somebody to find him. I had to survive. I knew I had enough fuel for thirty minutes.

As I came out of the bottom of the clouds, I saw the grey sea below me. I also saw a military helicopter. I waited until I was just above the sea, then I jumped. The water was icy. I spun deep into it, then my life jacket brought me back up to the surface. I turned and watched the balloon. Without my weight it quietly rose back up through the cloud and disappeared.

The helicopter flew over me and picked me up. 'Where's Per?' I asked the pilot. 'Have you picked up Per yet?'

'Isn't he in the balloon?'

'Haven't you got him? He's in the water. He's been there about forty minutes.'

Within two minutes we had landed on a ship. The pilot took off again immediately and flew back over the sea. For twenty minutes we heard nothing. Then we heard the pilot over the radio. 'We've seen him and he's still swimming. He's alive.'

When he was rescued, Per was almost dead. He had been in the water for two hours and he was very cold and exhausted.

We met on board the ship and fell into each other's arms. We were the first people to cross the Atlantic in a hot-air balloon. We couldn't believe that we had both survived.

Chapter 9   'Everything was up for sale.' 1988–1990

During the summer of 1987, British Caledonian had struggled to stay in business. They were losing money, and in August they announced that British Airways would take them over. We complained that this deal increased BA's share from 45 per cent to 80 per cent on several routes across the Atlantic, but the deal was still approved. Although a larger BA was a threat to us, it could also contain a hidden opportunity. We had already rented a second plane which we were flying to Miami. We wanted to expand further. The aviation rules said that there could be two British airlines flying between the US and Britain. With B-Cal removed from the scene, Virgin Atlantic could apply to fly the routes as the second of these airlines.

We continued talking to Thorn EMI, but we decided to buy 5 per cent of the company before announcing our bid. By the second week of October 1987, our shares had cost £30 million.

On Friday 16 October, the Wall Street stock market crashed. The effect of this did not hit London and the rest of the world until Monday. I thought that this was a good opportunity to buy more shares, and I called up our dealer and asked him to buy £5 million of Thorn EMI shares. I wanted to get them before anybody else. The dealer did this within twenty seconds and asked me if I wanted to buy more.

Finally sensing a crisis, I paused. Within minutes, the London stock market fell by 100 points, then another 100 points, then another 50 points. Within a three-day period, the world stock markets lost a quarter of their value.

For me the immediate problem was that the price of Virgin shares dropped from 160 pence to 90 pence. The share price of Thorn EMI dropped by over 20 per cent.

The Bank of Nova Scotia was not amused. With the fall in share prices, they asked for an immediate payment of £5 million. Strangely, I was still confident about buying Thorn EMI.

That week I had a serious argument with two directors who represented the outside shareholders' interests. 'There could be tough times ahead,' they warned me. 'This crash has changed the whole picture.'

'But the people who buy records won't stop,' I said.

The Thorn EMI share price continued to fall. I argued that this was a unique buying opportunity, but the directors disagreed with me and I had to let the matter drop.

The stock market crash ended Virgin's life as a public company. In July 1988 we announced that the management of Virgin would buy the company. We offered the same price that we had sold the shares for on the stock market so that nobody who had invested in Virgin – all those people in the queue outside the bank who had wished me well – would lose money.

A group of banks provided us with an overdraft of £300 million. We were heavily in debt and we had to move quickly to survive. We had to give up the idea of buying Thorn EMI, so we sold our shares and concentrated on our own problems. Trevor and I started looking for other companies that might wish to invest in Virgin. We wanted to replace the shareholders in the City with one or two key partners. The management of the Virgin Group was going to become very complicated.

◆

From the beginning, in 1971, Virgin had never made much profit from our record shops. After Nik left in 1980, nobody had organized them effectively. When Don Cruickshank carried out a review of the company, it became clear that retailing was not making us any money.

'Let's sell them all,' I said. After second thoughts, I wondered whether we should sell the smaller record shops and keep the Megastores. I had two reasons for changing my mind. The world's largest record store, owned by HMV, had actually increased record sales in Oxford Street; and secondly, Patrick had found a building in Paris that he wanted to turn into a Virgin Megastore.

In June 1988, we sold sixty-seven of the smaller stores to WH Smith, who renamed them Our Price Records. Trevor and I then divided Virgin Retail into three separate divisions. The first division consisted of the record shops that we had not sold to WH Smith, and the Oxford Street Megastore; the second was

Patrick Zelnick's proposed Paris Megastore; the third consisted of the plans we had for Ian Duffell, the man who had designed and set up the HMV shop on Oxford Street. We persuaded him to join Virgin. He was one of the best record retailers in the business and he planned to open more overseas Virgin Megastores.

Patrick's Paris Megastore was a great success and became the most famous shop in Paris. Today it still has sales per square metre of twice those of any other record store in the world. But I still had no idea what to do about the British record shops, so we decided to bring some other people in to improve Virgin Retail.

One of the applicants for the job of chief executive was Simon Burke. He had joined Virgin a couple of years previously as the development manager. Although he had no formal qualifications to turn a large number of unsuccessful record shops into successful ones, I was certain that he could do it. As soon as he started work in August 1988, things began to change.

Simon's first move was to clean out all the rubbish in the stores. We were selling a wide range of goods, from American football equipment to greeting cards, and he got rid of them all. His plan began to work, and by June 1989 Virgin Retail had produced its first profit. He asked the board for £10 million to invest in new shops. To create the investment for the UK shops, we sold 50 per cent of our ten UK Megastores to WH Smith. Unlike the earlier shops we had sold to WH Smith, they continued to trade under the Virgin name. Simon suddenly found himself with a new boss: a two-headed creature consisting of both Virgin and WH Smith.

♦

While many British companies complain about how difficult it is to do business in Japan, Virgin has always enjoyed an excellent relationship with the Japanese. By 1988 we had become quite a well-known brand name in Japan. Several of our artists sold well there, particularly Boy George, The Human League and Phil Collins. After the British Airways take-over of British Caledonian, we successfully applied to fly to Tokyo. When we looked at ways to reduce our overdraft, we realized that we would have to sell shares in both Virgin Atlantic and Virgin Music to reduce our debts.

We sold 10 per cent of the airline to Seibu-Saison, a large Japanese travel group, for £36 million. At the same time, we signed a long-term contract with Sega for Virgin Communications to distribute Sega games. It was clear that Japanese companies shared the same philosophy as Virgin. Like us they prefer to operate on long-term goals.

The next part of the Virgin Group to take a Japanese partner was Virgin Music. Simon, Trevor and I spoke to a number of American companies about buying a share in Virgin Music. One of them offered the most money, but was not prepared to be a silent, long-term investor. We chose a Japanese media company, Fujisankei. I think I made the decision at a meeting with one of its executives.

'Mr Branson,' came the quiet question. 'Would you prefer an American wife or a Japanese wife? American wives are very difficult – Japanese wives are very good and quiet.'

We sold 25 per cent of Virgin Music for $150 million. With Japanese partners in our two main businesses, the airline and music, we then turned to our third business and decided to expand the retail side in Japan as well.

We knew that our competitors were losing money in Tokyo because they had to pay a lot for their shops, and also because they had not built any customer loyalty. To avoid this problem, we set up a deal with the retailer Marui, who found an excellent site in the best shopping area in central Tokyo. The Tokyo Virgin Megastore soon acquired the same reputation as the early shops in London. It became the most popular place to go for teenagers from across the city.

Within two years, between 1988 and 1990, we were ready to expand in Japan. I was also planning a different kind of project there: Per and I were going to take off from Japan and fly across the Pacific to the US in our second hot-air balloon adventure.

♦

We were attempting the flight in November, when the ocean is extremely stormy. We would take off from Japan and almost immediately be above the sea. We would then have to more than double our Atlantic distance record of 4,800 kilometres in order to reach the US.

Per's team had taken the balloon to Miyakonojo, a small town in the south of Japan. The atmosphere there was almost like a festival. My parents arrived, but Joan chose to stay at home until the balloon went up. She would then take a plane to Los Angeles so that she and the children could meet me at the end of the flight.

We were delayed twice by the weather. The next time we went to the site, a crowd of 5,000 people had come to watch in the freezing cold. The wind was still but we needed to take off as soon as possible.

I was standing with my parents admiring the balloon when a piece of fabric suddenly came off the outside of the balloon and hung down.

'What's that?' Dad asked me.

I ran to find Per. 'Nothing to worry about,' he said. 'Just air coming up the side of the balloon. It will be OK.'

Dad didn't believe him. Per and I walked out and stood underneath the balloon. It had a hole in it. We went back into the control room.

'You can't fly in that thing,' Dad said. A minute later, more pieces of fabric started falling off.

'Richard, I'm afraid we're going to have to abandon the flight,' Per said. 'If we take off, we'll end up in the Pacific.'

I looked at the crowd on the hillside. I was going to disappoint them. As I spoke to them through a microphone, three or four huge pieces of fabric crashed off the balloon. It was falling apart in front of our eyes.

'We'll come back next year,' I promised.

'Well, Richard,' Dad said, as we drove back to the hotel, 'holidays with you are never boring.'

Joan had started her flight to Los Angeles when she heard the news. 'Excellent!' she cried. 'Drinks for everyone, please!'

In December 1990, Per and I tried once again to cross the Pacific in a hot-air balloon. This time we succeeded. We flew for 46 hours and 6 minutes and covered nearly 9,000 kilometres. It was further than any balloon had ever flown.

Chapter 10   'Who the hell does Richard Branson think he is?' 1990–1991

I was woken by a kick in my back. It was 5.30 a.m., so I got out of bed and watched Sam curl up on my warm pillow. He and Holly often slept in our bed with us. I turned on the television and listened to the news. Iraqi soldiers had marched into Kuwait the previous week. The price of oil and aviation fuel had gone up dramatically.

Two things that make an airline profitable are the number of passengers and the cost of aviation fuel. In the first week after the Iraqis took Kuwait, more than 3,000 people cancelled flights.

In the summer of 1990 Virgin Atlantic was still a tiny airline. We flew to four cities in two countries. The Tokyo route was the worst affected. We were allowed to fly only four times a week –

and never on Sunday, which is the most popular day for businessmen to travel – so the route was already losing money.

We had celebrated my fortieth birthday the previous month. Although Joan organized a wonderful party on Necker, I was depressed. It was very hard negotiating every contract and repeatedly talking about the same issues. What was I doing with my life? I found that it was difficult to develop the airline as quickly as I wanted. We could only fly out of Gatwick Airport, we were struggling to make money and we were arguing with British Airways. Should I start doing something completely different?

All these thoughts were forgotten when Saddam Hussein attacked Kuwait, and I found myself involved in the Gulf War in a very personal way.

My friendship with Queen Noor of Jordan was one of the unlikely results of my balloon trip across the Atlantic. She had asked me to teach her and her family to fly a balloon and I spent a week with them at King Hussein's palace.

Many foreign workers left Iraq for Jordan. There were about 150,000 refugees in a camp with no water and no blankets. When I heard about this, I contacted King Hussein and Queen Noor and offered to help. Queen Noor said that the Red Cross was trying to find 100,000 blankets.

Virgin Atlantic agreed to provide the plane to take the blankets to Amman. The Red Cross appealed on national radio and blankets started arriving at Gatwick. Two days later, all the seats were removed from one of our planes and replaced by over 40,000 blankets, rice and medical supplies. The plane flew to Amman and came back with some British citizens who had been in Jordan and wanted to come home.

When I returned to Britain, the politician William Waldegrave told me that Lord King, chairman of British Airways, had been surprised to see the Virgin Atlantic flight on the television news. 'We should be doing that,' Lord King told Waldegrave.

The next week British Airways flew more supplies to Jordan and brought back some more British citizens. The charity Christian Aid told us that they were amazed: for many years they had unsuccessfully asked British Airways to help them. Healthy competition benefits charities sometimes.

A few days later I was watching the news when I saw pictures of Saddam Hussein surrounded by Britons who had been kept in Baghdad. I had to do something to help these people. If we could get permission to fly to Baghdad, we could pick up any people whom Saddam Hussein agreed to release.

I spent the next three days in Amman with King Hussein and Queen Noor, and I learnt how a businessman can help during a crisis. Through King Hussein, I could contact Saddam Hussein.

I wrote a letter to him. I told him that I was staying in Amman, helping to take refugees home and organizing some medical and food supplies. I asked if he would release any foreigners who were caught in Baghdad, particularly women, children and sick people. King Hussein translated my letter into Arabic and wrote a letter to accompany it.

Two nights after I returned to England, Saddam Hussein replied. He promised to release the women, children and the sick, but he wanted somebody important to ask him publicly to do so. I telephoned Edward Heath, the former leader of the British government, and he agreed. The next day we flew Edward Heath to Amman and King Hussein arranged for him to go to Baghdad.

A day later King Hussein said, 'I have good news for you. You can go to Baghdad. Saddam promises that you will be safe.'

We had a brave volunteer crew. When I warned the other Virgin directors, they were understandably concerned. They knew that if the plane was delayed in Baghdad for more than a few days we could go bankrupt. I was risking everything on this flight, but I also knew that we had to do it.

When we arrived at Baghdad airport, we were taken into a bare departure lounge where all the computers, telephones and lights had been taken out. We handed out some gifts we'd brought: chocolates and children's games. Then I heard a movement and Edward Heath came out at the head of a large crowd of men, women and children. As soon as they saw us they cheered.

I realized that we couldn't take all these people back with us. A pregnant Filipino woman who was leaving her husband came up to me. She was crying. Another man had to say goodbye to his three-year-old daughter. I put my arms around him. There was nothing else I could do. We both had tears in our eyes. I was a father too.

After half an hour the Iraqis told us to get back on the plane. We were probably the first Westerners they had ever met. They knew that more would soon arrive, dropping bombs.

When the plane took off, the party started. People clapped when the pilot announced that we had left Iraqi airspace. Two months later Baghdad airport was reduced to dust by the heaviest bombing ever used by a military force.

'Who does Richard Branson think he is?' Lord King demanded in a second phone call to William Waldegrave.

That question was repeated by some newspapers, which suggested that I was doing it for personal gain. I tried to analyse my motives for doing things in my diary. Did I need recognition? I don't think so. The problem is that you have to use yourself publicly to get attention. Television is very powerful. Because I spoke on TV, medicine, food, blankets and tents reached the refugees. I believe that by moving quickly a major disaster was avoided.

The question is how often someone can use the press in this way without losing public support. If there was a suggestion that I did it for fame, then I wouldn't be able to do it at all.

I didn't know that the Virgin flight into Baghdad would annoy Lord King. I found out later that his reaction was the start of a campaign by British Airways to put Virgin Atlantic out of business.

♦

Friday 25 January 1991 was the end of a bad week for Sidney Shaw, our account director from Lloyds Bank.

'I saw Air Europe on Monday and Dan Air on Wednesday,' he began, 'and I suspect that you have the same problems. I'm afraid that we're taking back our loans from both those airlines. I don't think we should support you any more. We can't see how you can keep Virgin Atlantic going.'

He had come to see us in the worst week in the worst year of aviation history. Virgin's overdraft with Lloyds Bank had gone up to £50 million. The Gulf War continued, the price of aviation fuel was still high and passengers were still not flying. To an outsider, the airline industry looked like a disaster. For the rest of the Virgin Group, though, the picture was good. Virgin Communications would reach sales of over £150 million that year on Sega equipment. Simon and Ken were having no problems selling records. The Virgin Megastores weren't making much money, but they weren't losing anything either.

Virgin Atlantic was our biggest problem, but even here the picture was encouraging. We thought that we would increase the number of holidays we sold through Virgin Holidays, and the amount we were paid for flying goods to Japan had actually increased.

'Look,' I told Sidney Shaw. 'We have a very secure business. With the Gulf War and the winter, we've got a cash shortage of £10–£20 million. This is a tiny percentage of the total value of the Virgin Group. Anyway, we could easily sell some or all of Virgin Music – and it's worth about $900 million.'

When Sidney Shaw walked away from the office, he seemed less worried. For the moment Lloyds Bank was supporting us. Unfortunately, they now had the idea that we could sell part or all of Virgin Music.

In London, rumours were going round the City that Virgin was having problems like Air Europe and Dan Air. I knew a lot of journalists, and I started receiving calls from them asking me whether there was a drugs problem at Heaven, our nightclub, and about the finances of Virgin Atlantic. I was confused. I felt that something strange was happening and that there must be some kind of campaign against us.

The news from the airline was also disturbing: the number of passengers who reserved seats and then didn't take them had increased dramatically.

One day Will came into my office looking worried. He told me that he'd heard Lord King was saying bad things about Virgin Atlantic.

An accusation of financial weakness can rapidly come true, particularly when it comes from a source like Lord King, who could talk to the press and the bankers in the City. Rumours that we were in financial trouble would stop banks investing in us. The third audience was the aircraft manufacturers: we wanted to expand, but nobody would do business with an airline that was in trouble. The last audience was the most important: the Civil Aviation Authority, which has to check that all airline companies have enough money to operate.

For two years we had been involved in an argument with BA about some work it had done on our planes. When we set up Virgin Atlantic, B-Cal did our engineering work. When British Airways took over B-Cal, they promised that they would continue the work. However, when we bought our third and fourth planes in September 1988, British Airways increased their labour costs from £16 to £61 per hour. Although it was expensive and inconvenient, we had to fly our planes to Ireland so that Aer Lingus could maintain them instead.

The other part of our argument started in the summer of 1988 when BA engineers failed to notice a crack in the link between the engine and the wing of one of our aircraft. The plane couldn't fly and BA refused to let us have one of their aircraft to replace it. We couldn't fly for sixteen days in August, the busiest time of the year.

I called Sir Colin Marshall, chief executive of BA. 'Your engineering was so bad that it could have brought an aircraft down,' I told him.

'That's one of the dangers of being in the aviation business,' he said coldly. 'If you'd stayed in popular music you wouldn't have had this problem. No, we won't lend you a plane.'

We lost money because we had to rent a replacement aircraft. When we tried to get compensation, BA was slow to agree. They owed us several million pounds, and by delaying payment they started a cash crisis at the airline.

We also had a battle with British Airways over our application for two extra flights a week to Japan. We needed to fly daily, and from Heathrow. When news of our application came out, British Airways were very angry. Lord King and his team argued that British Airways had a right to these slots.

'They're not "your" slots,' Malcolm Rifkind, the minister for transport told them. 'They belong to the government and we issue them to you. BA does not own them.'

British Airways said that Virgin Atlantic was not financially strong enough to take these slots. They also wrote to the Department of Transport about our finances. The CAA could not give the slots to Virgin Atlantic if we were going bankrupt.

Finally, in the last week of January, the CAA made two decisions in our favour: it gave the two extra slots to Virgin Atlantic and recommended that we should operate from Heathrow.

On 29 January the first television programme about Virgin Atlantic and British Airways was shown. It described the battle we were having. The next day British Airways told the press that we were abusing them.

I continued to hear damaging rumours. On 31 January, I wrote my first letter to Lord King. I believe that personal relationships are important in business and that people should be responsible for their actions. I hoped that Lord King would call me and we could sort the matter out.

My letter didn't help. The next week Will was called by a private detective, Frank Dobson. He told us that a detective agency, Kroll Associates, was investigating me and the whole Virgin Group. He asked if he could work for Virgin. Will thanked him for his information, but turned down the offer of help because we never use private detectives.

I received Lord King's reply to my letter on 5 February, quoting a comment he had made to a newspaper: 'I run my airline; Richard Branson runs his. Best of luck to him.' He added that he intended to say nothing more on the subject.

Lord King did not want me to have the 'best of luck'. And he would go on to say a lot more about 'the subject' to a number of people.

Chapter 11   Dirty tricks 1991

After the television programme, we had more proof of a campaign against me and Virgin.

'I've had a call from an ex-British Airways man,' Chris Moss, our marketing manager, told me. 'He says that after the Baghdad flight, BA set up a special team to attack you.'

'Can you get it in writing?'

'I'll try.'

Throughout February and March we discussed with Malcolm Rifkind, the minister for transport, the flights to Tokyo and our plans to use Heathrow.

'Richard,' he said one day, 'you must admit that BA does an excellent job.'

'Yes, they've improved a lot,' I agreed. 'But they've had a lot of help. They use Heathrow.'

'It's good for the country,' Rifkind said.

I disagreed and argued that British Airways was just a large airline which was owned by its shareholders. I thought I had said too much. Malcolm Rifkind had never flown Virgin because all politicians were still encouraged to fly British Airways.

On 15 March 1991 Rifkind called me. 'Good news, Richard,' he said. 'I am pleased to say that the government will allow Virgin Atlantic to operate from Heathrow. And we're going to suggest that you get the two extra flights to Tokyo.'

As we celebrated, the telephone started ringing with calls from journalists who had heard the story. They were also calling Lord King. He said in an interview to the *Observer* newspaper, 'Every time we build up a profitable route, someone comes along and says "I'll have some of that", and the government lets them.' He estimated that Malcolm Rifkind's decision to allow Virgin to fly the two extra flights to Tokyo would cost BA about £250 million. 'That is £250 million ... which has gone straight into Richard Branson's back pocket.'

A letter from a British Airways employee, Peter Fleming, arrived on the following Monday. It said that a management team had been set up to destroy us, but relevant papers had been destroyed. I decided to take no action while we watched the British Airways 'dirty tricks' develop.

Meanwhile we had plenty to do. We needed to start operating from Heathrow. Everything was a battle. First we were told that there were no check-in desks available. When I walked around the airport, I saw a whole line of empty check-in desks. 'Whose are those?' I asked.

'British Airways', came the answer.

British Airways refused to rent them to us when they weren't using them. I appealed to the British Airports Authority and said that I was thinking about taking my complaints to the European Court. BAA eventually found us some check-in desks, but we weren't allowed to use our own luggage handlers and had to use British Midland's.

We applied for sixty-four slots when we could operate our flights to Los Angeles, Tokyo and New York from Heathrow. We were offered twenty-three, most of them at inconvenient times of the day. Some of them allowed us to take off, but not to land or return.

I complained to the Heathrow slot manager, Peter Morrisroe, an employee of British Airways.

'You didn't have to come to Heathrow,' he said. 'You could have stayed at Gatwick.'

I talked to lawyers about the slots. We decided that the system broke European Union competition law because it stopped new airlines competing at Heathrow.

Malcolm Rifkind had given three airlines, Virgin, American and United, permission to use Heathrow. All three airlines had to compete for very few slots. But when slots were available, the slot manager gave them to American and United rather than allowing us all to bid for them.

Finally, Peter Morrisroe agreed to meet me for lunch. I told him that what he had done was wrong. I also suggested that we force the government to take over and give out the Heathrow slots. I said that I would not involve the government if we could work out a timetable. Peter Morrisroe agreed. Virgin Atlantic was finally able to use Heathrow.

◆

While I was involved in my debate about the Heathrow slots, Jordan Harris and Jeff Ayerhoff, who ran our American record label, called me to say that Janet Jackson wanted to join Virgin Music. Janet Jackson was the world's top female singer and she wanted to be even more successful than her brother Michael.

Although Janet told me that she would like to come to Virgin, other companies were still bidding for her. Virgin would have to match the highest offer. It was going to cost more money than we had, but I knew that we had to have her.

Sometimes it is essential to spend a lot of money. After talking with Simon and Ken, I decided to offer Janet the largest amount of money ever offered to any singer. I also decided to break all the rules of the record industry: instead of giving her a contract for a number of albums, Virgin would offer her a contract for just one album. I was confident that when she started working with Virgin, she wouldn't want to go to another company.

Janet Jackson would also send out the right message to the people in the City and the CAA who believed the British Airways' rumour that the Virgin Group had a cash crisis.

But we *did* have a cash crisis. I knew that Lloyds Bank wouldn't extend our overdraft, so we looked for ways to raise more money. After some rapid meetings, the Bank of Nova Scotia agreed to pay for the Janet Jackson contract.

We offered Janet $15 million with a payment of $5 million when she signed the contract. However, the price soon rose to $25 million, just for one album. The Bank of Nova Scotia assured me that they would give us the $25 million.

Janet chose Virgin. The contract was ours and we had to find $11 million to pay her immediately.

I took the family and one of my closest friends, Peter Gabriel, on a skiing holiday. At the hotel, I received a phone call. It was Trevor.

'Bad news, I'm afraid. We can't get the money for Janet

Jackson. Nova Scotia have pulled out of the deal. We need $11 million by close of business in Los Angeles.'

I wasn't going to let our rivals have her. I knew that we were paying out about £5 million the following week on record sales to our musicians. We rapidly looked at a list of options: we could ask Fujisankei to put more money in Virgin Music; we could take some cash out of Virgin Communications; I could sell Necker Island. But all this would take time. We would have to go back to the Bank of Nova Scotia.

'Go and see the head of the bank in Toronto,' I said to Trevor.

'I could see Bruce Birmingham, the second in command,' Trevor said.

I called Ken in Los Angeles. 'Trevor's going to Toronto,' I told him. 'We're trying to get Nova Scotia back.'

'We must finalize the deal this evening,' Ken said.

By 3 a.m. the hotel was silent. I sat by the phone and waited. Finally, it rang: it was Trevor and Bruce calling me from the Bank of Nova Scotia. I promised that Virgin would sell as many copies of Janet Jackson's next album as her brother's album *Thriller* had sold.

'It's a matter of trust,' Trevor said to Bruce. 'Virgin has never let you down on any of our loan repayments. This will be no different.'

There was a long pause. 'They'll be angry with me in London,' Bruce finally said. 'But Janet Jackson's a great lady. Let's complete the deal. But I wouldn't do this for Madonna.'

It took another two hours to get the money, but finally it was handed over to Janet Jackson's lawyers.

We now needed to release some cash. Trevor and Robert sold the European licence to distribute Sega computer games back to the parent company, Sega in Japan, for £33 million.

Before the sale, Robert separated the small team who wrote the computer programmes into a separate company called Virgin Interactive. In 1990 the next wave of technology would be games which were played on CDs. The team began to develop a new game called 'The 7th Guest'. People were getting very excited about it.

'I've no idea what happens in this game. I'm always killed in the first room,' Robert told me. 'The team tells me that "The 7th Guest" is going to be big. They say it's much better than anything else on the market.'

◆

'Perhaps it was just a bad day but one of Virgin's passengers was clearly not impressed with the service in upper class last week. An entry in the visitors' book read: "No wonder your boss travels round the world in a balloon."'

This was a small article in the *Sunday Telegraph* by a journalist called Frank Kane. It sounded all wrong to me. We had so few passenger complaints that the crew would have told me about this one. I found the entry in the visitors' book. Frank Kane had missed out the last line: 'But seriously, I had a great time.'

I don't mind bad press if it is accurate, but clearly this was not. I contacted the passenger and she assured me she'd had a wonderful flight – it was just a joke. Then I wrote to the *Sunday Telegraph* and pointed out that Frank Kane had not quoted all of her comment. Worse still, a journalist then read the piece out on television. The damage was done. Six million viewers did not know that this comment was only part of the full story.

◆

I hid inside the van waiting for the signal. It was 4 a.m. on 7 July 1991, and we were parked outside Heathrow. We had put a red flag over the tail of Concorde, and boards stating VIRGIN TERRITORY nearby. I was dressed as a pirate with a toy parrot on one shoulder. We'd finally been let into Heathrow and we wanted the world to know. Soon the police came to see us.

'Everyone's having a good laugh, I see,' the policeman said. 'But British Airways has asked me to arrest you.'

'Are you arresting me then?' I asked.

'Of course not,' the policeman laughed. 'I told BA that nothing would please you more.'

I dressed up as a pirate because Lord King called me one. He felt that I was 'robbing' him of air routes and money that belonged to British Airways. One of the reasons I dress up is to give the press photographers a good picture that will promote the Virgin brand name.

Our sales on the three routes we offered from Heathrow rapidly increased by 15 per cent. On 14 July British Airways' internal magazine published an article that said we wanted to steal more slots and that it was unfair that a lower-priced competitor should be allowed to compete with them.

On 16 July Lord King announced that British Airways would stop giving money to the political party that ran the government. This revealed his belief that giving money in the past had gained them various privileges. BA's influence went further than just giving money. During the summer I talked to a group of politicians. Afterwards I had a drink with some of them and chatted about their holiday plans.

'Have you seen your travel agent yet?' one asked.

'No, I'm just going to call them to get my free ticket.'

'Who's this travel agent?' I asked.

'British Airways, of course,' they said together.

Despite the excitement of starting our Heathrow operation, it was clear that Virgin Atlantic would be unable to expand any further for some time. We didn't offer a new route for three years until we started flying to Hong Kong in 1994. This was because of one of the fiercest attacks ever started by an airline against a smaller competitor.

Chapter 12   'They're calling me a liar.' 1991–1992

In September 1991 everything started to go wrong. Finding money for the Janet Jackson deal had created difficulties for Virgin Music, and I was increasingly worried about Simon's commitment to the company. He had stopped going to clubs to search for new talent and Virgin had not found any significant new bands for a couple of years. He seemed more interested in his own personal projects than the business.

It was hard for Virgin Atlantic to compete with British Airways. Our engineering teams were now driving three or four times a day between Heathrow and Gatwick to maintain each flight. We heard that Lord King was telling people that Virgin was going bankrupt. BA was also stealing our passengers. We had two reports that BA called Virgin Atlantic passengers at home and tried to persuade them to change their flights from Virgin to BA. Our staff also saw BA staff approaching Virgin Atlantic passengers at the airport and trying to persuade them to change to BA.

I was the only person who was part of both Virgin Atlantic and Virgin Music. The only other thing that linked them was Lloyds Bank, because the loans that Lloyds had made to Virgin Atlantic were guaranteed by Virgin Music.

Our troubles at Virgin Atlantic made us think about the future of Virgin Music. I had put the idea of selling the record company to the back of my mind, but I realized that something had to be done.

When I set up the airline in 1984, I did so against Simon's wishes. Our friendship never fully recovered. Now, when Virgin Atlantic needed more investment, Simon didn't want to move money from Virgin Music to Virgin Atlantic. I wanted to sell part of Virgin Music to raise funds for Virgin Atlantic, but Simon wanted to sell the whole company. Ken told me he didn't mind what happened to Virgin Music because he would stay whatever happened. That made selling Virgin Music to another company easier: Ken would remain there to look after everyone, both the staff and the musicians. It soon became clear that Thorn EMI was very interested in buying Virgin Music.

I couldn't decide what to do. If we agreed to sell, we would have enough cash for Virgin Atlantic to survive through the winter. But we would be selling something that we had spent the best part of our lives building up. Everyone who worked at Virgin Music had become a close friend, and many of them had been there for over ten years. I wanted to wait until the last possible moment to make a decision, but our bankers were pushing us to sell.

♦

I was in Japan looking for a possible site for a Virgin Megastore in Kyoto. I took the train from Tokyo to Kyoto. It was rather like being on a plane: there was music to listen to, food and drink. 'Why can't trains be like this in the UK?' I wondered. I made some notes about trains in Britain and trains in Japan, and then turned my attention to the Megastore site.

Back in London the next week, a reporter from the *Sunday Telegraph* rang Will and asked if Virgin would be interested in operating trains if the government sold British Rail.

'Well, are we?' I asked.

'It's quite an interesting idea,' Will said. 'I love trains. And they could be run in a completely different way. We could give free meals, free newspapers, all the Virgin services. We could compete with British Airways on the London-to-Manchester and London-to-Glasgow routes. Maybe it would free some slots at Heathrow.'

'Tell him that we are,' I suggested. 'It can't do any harm.'

The *Sunday Telegraph* story read 'VIRGIN TO GO INTO TRAINS'. It became the story of the week.

We prepared a small business plan and talked to British Rail about running some of its trains, but they weren't keen. As he walked out of the office, John Welsby, the chief executive of British Rail, made a comment to his companions which was picked up on the loudspeaker and broadcast all over the office. He said that he'd be in his grave before I would get the Virgin name on his trains.

◆

Throughout the week of 21 October I replaced Angela Rippon on her early morning London radio show. The producer called Lord King and invited him on the show to debate the problems between British Airways and Virgin.

'Tell him we're not prepared to lower our standards that much,' Lord King said to her.

The previous week I had received a call from Joseph Campbell, who runs our company cars. 'I'm sorry to bother you,' he said, 'but I thought you should know that something rather strange has happened. One of my staff has a daughter who works for some private investigators. She says that the company is spying on you.'

I put the telephone down and looked at it. Was anyone listening to my calls? Were private detectives following my children to school? Maybe the van parked in the street was full of listening equipment. Then I pushed the thought from my mind. I couldn't change the way I lived, and I had nothing to hide.

At the end of the week I had a call from Chris Hutchins, a reporter with *Today* newspaper. 'I've spoken to Brian Basham,' he said.

'Who's he?'

'BA's public relations man. I know Basham's wife quite well and she called me to say that Brian might have a good story about Branson and drugs . . . I called Basham and he told me he'd been doing a detailed study for BA on Virgin operations, its strengths and weaknesses. He also mentioned a story about Heaven and suggested that I check the drugs position there myself.'

'Will you come and see me at the weekend?' I asked. 'I'd like to talk to you about this.'

I asked Will if he had heard of Brian Basham. 'He's bad news,' Will said. He told me that Basham had a lot of influence and close links with the newspaper industry.

The phone rang again. It was a reporter from *The Times*. He'd heard that we were making a lot of staff redundant. The *Sunday Telegraph* was the next to phone. The journalist would not reveal where his information had come from.

Another call came through. It was Sir Freddie Laker. 'Hi Richard,' he said cheerfully. 'Just a quick call to remind you that it is exactly ten years since British Airways put me out of business. I've heard about your problems with BA. You've got to deal with them before it's too late. Sue them!'

With this shout ringing in our ears, Will and I went to the television studios where I was doing a live interview with talk-show host Clive Anderson. Anderson began attacking Virgin Atlantic. I started to answer his questions, but he wasn't interested. I stared at him with growing anger. You can laugh at me as much as you like, I thought, but I've worked hard for twenty years to build up one of the biggest private companies in the country. I scarcely heard the rest of Clive Anderson's comments. I smiled at him, stood up, picked up my glass of water and poured it over his head. I then walked out of the studio and into the street to get some fresh air.

'Oh, well,' Clive Anderson said, wiping his hair and jacket. 'I've only got one thing to say to that: fly British Airways.'

◆

Chris Hutchins came to see me on Sunday 27 October 1991, and I sensed that he was worried. The following day he was going to lunch with Brian Basham. I wanted him to take a hidden microphone to record whatever Brian Basham had to say. I also wanted Chris to give me a copy of the telephone conversation he'd had with Brian Basham on Thursday. He didn't want to do either.

'Look at what BA are doing,' I said to him. 'This could destroy our business. I need someone to help me or Virgin Atlantic will go bankrupt and thousands of people will be out of work. Why did you call me about Brian Basham if you now say you can't help me?'

'I called you because I thought that what BA was doing was wrong. But I don't think I could secretly record him.'

We sat in silence. I just looked at Chris as he decided what to do.

'All right,' he finally agreed.

I went through a list of questions I wanted Chris to ask. Will bought a tiny tape recorder and showed Chris how to work it. I spoke to Martin Dunn, the editor of *Today*, and told him what Chris was going to do. Martin confirmed that he was happy for Chris to go in with the hidden tape recorder. Things were building up to a crisis.

When Chris came back to see me, I could see that he was embarrassed. He didn't want to give me either the tape or the report of the investigation on Virgin that Basham had given to him. I made him a cup of tea and smiled encouragingly. He was not walking out of my house with either the tape or the report.

'So what happened?'

'Well, I brought you a couple of things . . .'

'What did you bring?' I asked pleasantly.

'I brought a copy of my first conversation with Basham, and also the tape and Basham's report.'

'Let's have a look at the conversation first.'

Chris pushed over a piece of paper. Its title was 'Chris Hutchins' conversation with Brain Basham in a telephone call which started at 1.40 p.m. Thursday 24 October'. I read that Basham said drugs were apparently available at Heaven. His client, British Airways, wanted to know more about Virgin and my cash position. Hutchins asked why Basham didn't investigate Virgin himself. Basham said that his client didn't want to appear to be involved if I went out of business.

Chris gave me the tape and I played it. The quality was very poor and I only heard a few words. The clearest part of the recording was hearing Chris use the toilet. Then it stopped. This tape wasn't going to ruin British Airways.

'I'll take the tape to our sound engineers and see if they can make it clearer,' I said. Chris agreed. I turned to Basham's report. The first section listed our strengths and weaknesses. I turned the page and read a description of myself. It said that my business methods were very experimental. Although I had been able to get out of unsuccessful projects in the past, I might not be able to in the future. If my Japanese investors lost confidence in me, it would be a disaster. It said that I loved publicity and got bored easily. It also mentioned that Heaven nightclub might be a centre for drugs.

'Will *Today* reveal BA's actions?' I asked.

'I'll have to talk to our editor, Martin Dunn.' Chris didn't seem enthusiastic and I wondered if he was unhappy about betraying Basham. We agreed that we'd talk after he had spoken to Martin Dunn, and I'd examine the tape again to see if we could make it clearer.

An hour later, Will and I were in the studios. Two engineers played with the controls and suddenly we heard Basham's voice. To be fair, Basham later claimed that his role in the whole dirty tricks affair was misrepresented by BA, who were happy to blame others for their activities. He said that I had a lot of schemes, and some of them needed a lot of capital. He said that I always worked with the minimum of cash and just before I ran out of money I refinanced. Basham thought that two things could ruin me. The first was the ballooning; if anything went wrong, Virgin would fall apart because it was my charm that brought money into the business. The second was Heaven, because there was always the risk of a drugs problem in a nightclub. Basham also criticised the government's decision to allow Virgin to fly to Tokyo. He had been told, he said, that the business was badly run, which would become clear when an aircraft fell out of the sky, as aircraft did.

'First of all, I don't want to be involved in this at all,' Basham said. 'Secondly, I mustn't have BA involved in this at all. All the good I might have done by saying, "Here is Virgin, good and bad," would be wiped out if it looked as if BA was running a campaign against Virgin – which they're not.'

'It's not going to get you in trouble with Lord King, is it, if we attack Branson?' Chris asked.

'No,' Basham said. 'It doesn't make any difference to me as long as neither BA nor I are linked with it.'

Will and I looked at each other. 'Well, I'm afraid that both you and BA are going to be linked with it,' I said. I wondered what to do with the tape. I felt as if I had just witnessed a crime, and I was the victim. We sent a copy of the tape round to Gerrard Tyrrell, our lawyer.

Things moved quickly that week. Chris Hutchins called to say that his editor was investigating the story and would print it on the front cover of *Today*. However, they began to worry about checking BA's side of the story, and nothing appeared in the newspaper.

We also discovered that British Airways was getting information about our passengers and contacting them. That was confirmed in a second letter from Peter Fleming. He said that when Virgin went to the European Court, he was told to destroy all documents that referred to Virgin. He listed more details. British Airways had applied for slots to Japan and Australia that it didn't need just to stop Virgin getting them. It had set up a special sales team to get business in the Gatwick area. It had refused to process bookings for passengers who had flown from Japan to Gatwick by Virgin and wanted to switch to BA, and it had taken information from the computer booking system.

The *Sunday Times* reporter Nick Rufford was investigating a story about Virgin and had called Brian Basham and recorded the conversation. Basham suggested that Virgin had to pay cash in advance for its airline fuel. When Rufford called Will to get a response to the story, Will was very angry.

'That's nonsense,' he said. 'If the newspapers print that about a small airline we'll go out of business.'

I spoke to Rufford and told him the story was rubbish: I did not have to pay cash for my fuel.

'Why don't you write about British Airways' dirty tricks instead?' I suggested. 'That's the real story.'

'I could try that,' Rufford said. 'What evidence do you have?'

'I don't know where to begin,' I said, thinking of the Basham tape which *Today* had still not used.

'BRANSON ATTACKS BA "TRICKS"' was on the front page of the *Sunday Times* on 3 November 1991. For the first time Brian Basham was publicly linked with BA. Rufford reported that Basham had given his secret report to a number of journalists.

Today finally decided to print their own story the next day. The editor called me. 'Basham has gone mad. It's got very nasty.' But in the end *Today* decided not to print the story, giving in to pressure from BA.

I expected a lot of journalists to call me after the *Sunday Times* article, but the phone was strangely quiet. I didn't know what was going on.

◆

Despite the newspaper articles, the dirty tricks continued. British Airways ignored my accusations. I was desperate and began to look for any legal action we could take against them.

I didn't want to take British Airways to court. I knew that it would be expensive and risky, and that they would employ top lawyers to try and defeat us. I simply wanted the dirty tricks to stop. I looked for other ways to persuade them to end their campaign.

I wrote to some of the directors about the press campaign, engineering matters, sales and marketing and private investigators(?). I put a question mark on the final category since I still found it impossible to believe. I was certain that the directors couldn't ignore the evidence I sent them. Since they were responsible to their shareholders, we released copies of this letter to the press so that their shareholders could read it too.

To my surprise, two of the directors replied the next day denying my claims. They replied so quickly that they couldn't have investigated the contents of the letter. I now had to go forward. Unless British Airways apologized and put an end to their dirty tricks, I would have to take legal action.

The argument between us had one immediate result: Virgin Atlantic was unable to raise any money. One of British Airways' aims was to stop me expanding. The only way I could expand was by refinancing the airline. Nobody wanted to invest in an airline that might start a long and expensive court case against one of the world's largest airlines.

On 21 December a letter arrived from Lloyds Bank reminding us that we had exceeded our £55 million overdraft. We talked about where we could find enough funds to repay some of the bank debt. Virgin Music was our only seriously profitable business, and it was our only chance to save the airline. We started talking to several companies, including Thorn EMI, that were interested in acquiring Virgin Music.

The pressure from Lloyds continued and they clearly expected us to sell Virgin Music immediately. We knew that Virgin Music had sales of £330 million, making a profit of £38 million. Next year we were forecasting a profit of £75 million. But Lloyds would not wait.

A second television programme about the battle between British Airways and Virgin Atlantic was broadcast at the end of February. Will and I met the producer, Martyn Gregory, and told him as much as we could about British Airways, then left him to carry out his own independent investigation. British Airways refused to take part in the programme. Nothing could annoy an independent television producer more.

The programme interviewed Peter Fleming and he described the special unit BA set up to attack me. Someone else talked about BA approaching our passengers, and a Los Angeles travel agent described how passengers were switching to BA because they had heard that Virgin was going out of business. I was interviewed and said that many of the stories came from Brian Basham, who was employed by British Airways and reported to David Burnside, their head of publicity. Burnside reported directly to Lord King.

The film was seen by over seven million viewers and that evening we received more than 400 calls. Most people wished us well and said that they would never fly BA again. Some of them also had stories about British Airways approaching them at the airport as they tried to take a Virgin flight.

I wrote and asked the directors of BA to reconsider my previous letter and to make sure that their activities against Virgin stopped.

On Friday Will rang me from Gatwick Airport. He had a copy of *BA News*. The front-page story said that my dirty tricks claim was untrue. They said that I had lied. This was libel.

We contacted our lawyer, who agreed that BA had libelled me. Libel would be a much easier case to bring to court than a complicated case about BA abusing its power at Heathrow. It would also make everything public.

On Monday morning I discovered that Lord King had written personal letters to any viewers who had written to question British Airways' dirty tricks. He'd assured them that there was no truth in the accusations. He had repeated the same libel, and once again to members of the public. I decided that I should sue Lord King as well.

Chapter 13   Victory 1992–1993

We had been offered £560 million ($1 billion) for Virgin Music, but I didn't want it. I looked at Simon and Ken. We had spent the last twenty years building up the company. From being a small label back in 1973, we were now the label of choice for many of the world's biggest bands. But it was over.

'Ken?' I asked.

'It's your choice,' he said.

'Simon?'

'Take the cash. You've got no option.'

When anyone tells me that I've got no option, I try to prove them wrong. Over the last few days, Thorn EMI's offer had changed from offering shares which would have made me the largest shareholder in Thorn EMI to a higher cash offer. I was more attracted to the share exchange because I could use that in the future as the basis to bid for the company. But everyone told me it would be too risky to use these shares as a basis to borrow more money to support Virgin Atlantic. I had to change my mind and take the cash offer.

Before finally agreeing, I called Peter Gabriel. 'Don't do it, Richard,' he said. 'You'll never get it back again.'

I knew that he was right. But the pressure from BA was too great and I felt sure that Lloyds was going to ask for its overdraft to be repaid. I knew that Simon wanted to sell and take cash rather than maintain his involvement with Virgin by taking shares. My main aim was to save Virgin Atlantic. If I sold Virgin Music, the Virgin name would be saved. Instead of one struggling airline and a record company, there would be a secure airline and a secure record company – although it would be owned by Thorn EMI. I could stay on as president of the company. Most importantly, Ken would stay in charge of Virgin within EMI, and he would take care of the Virgin reputation.

'I'll take the cash,' I heard myself say.

Although I had saved the airline, I felt that I had killed something inside me. I was sad that Simon, Ken and I would go in separate directions. I knew that as soon as Virgin Music had gone, I would have to fight British Airways.

The next morning Thorn EMI announced the purchase of Virgin Music for exactly $1 billion – or £560 million. Simon, Ken and I went to see the staff at our Harrow Road offices. It felt like the death of a child. Simon, Ken and I had started Virgin and kept it going through all the bad times. We reinvented it with every new style of music so that it continued to be the most exciting record label in the business.

Ken told everyone that they would become part of Thorn EMI. Simon started to speak, but instead began to cry. Everyone looked at me. I was close to tears myself. I couldn't tell them the real reason why their company had been sold. If I told them the truth about the bank's attitude to Virgin Atlantic, the airline and the rest of the Virgin companies would be damaged by lack of confidence. Airlines are built on confidence, and admitting weakness would frighten away customers. I offered everyone a job at Virgin Atlantic if they were unhappy with EMI, and assured them that Ken would look after them. When there was a vote of thanks from the staff to me, Simon and Ken for 'the best years of our lives', I could bear it no longer. I left the room and ran down the road, tears streaming down my face.

Simon and Ken took their share of the money and went their separate ways. I used my money to repay the bank and invested the rest in Virgin Atlantic. We now had more cash to spend than British Airways.

The banks immediately started calling me – not to demand their money back, but to offer to look after my money. They offered to lend me as much money as I wanted to finance future deals!

It took some time for me to understand the full effects of the sale. For the first time in my life, I had enough money to satisfy my wildest dreams. But I had no time to think about it because that week British Airways again took all my attention.

On Friday 13 March Chris Moss, Virgin Atlantic's marketing director, received a tape recording in a brown envelope. It was of two men talking. One of them was Sir Colin Marshall, chief executive of BA, and he was talking about taking the television producers to court for their programme about Virgin and BA. Somebody had listened to British Airways' phones and sent the tape to us. I asked Chris to send the tape to me. Would this help – or was it a trap? I decided to send the tape back to British Airways for the personal attention of Sir Colin Marshall.

The next day Frank Kane rang me.

'I hear you've employed private detectives to investigate British Airways,' he said. 'I've also got proof that you've been listening to their phone conversations.'

'That's ridiculous, Frank,' I said. 'If you publish that story, then

I'll sue you.' I felt helpless. I knew that Frank Kane's story would damage our reputation. I was going to tell him about the tape we had received, but something stopped me. If I told Frank Kane about it, he could describe Sir Colin Marshall as the victim of a spying operation. Nobody would believe that we hadn't listened to his phone calls.

I called the editor of the *Sunday Telegraph*. 'This is a crazy story,' I said. 'You can't publish it. Tell Frank Kane to check his information again.'

I called my lawyer, Gerrard Tyrrell, and asked if we should get the courts to prevent the *Sunday Telegraph* publishing the story.

'Do you have a tape?' he asked.

'It's either at my house or we have already sent it to Colin Marshall. I haven't heard it myself.'

'I think the best thing to do is to threaten them with the courts and see what they do. This is very, very dangerous.'

I was curious and I fell into a trap. I had the tape in my possession. Whoever sent it knew that I would want to listen to it.

Later in the afternoon we had the first signs that the *Sunday Telegraph* would not publish the story. I repeatedly asked the editor for proof that I'd spied on BA, and Gerrard Tyrrell promised that we would sue them if the story was published without proper evidence. Hopefully honourable behaviour would stop them printing the story.

On Sunday 15 March I read the article in the *Sunday Telegraph*. There was no mention of detectives or spying. The following morning I wrote to Colin Marshall and enclosed the tape. I said that I didn't know where it came from. I didn't know who in British Airways was supplying misinformation about us, but I wanted them to stop. That afternoon Joan Thirkettle from a television news programme called me. 'I tried to get Lord King on television to debate the dirty tricks with you,' she said.

'Did he agree?' I asked.

'No, he said that he didn't debate with losers.'

I'd had enough.

I wrote to Lord King. I gave him until Wednesday 18 March to withdraw his statements that I had lied about BA to get publicity. I also demanded an apology.

I knew that he would never apologize. I would have to go to court to protect my reputation. I was sure we would win, but the law courts are rarely reliable. If I lost, then Virgin Atlantic would probably go out of business. My reputation would be ruined and everyone would turn against us.

By 6 p.m. on Wednesday I hadn't heard anything from BA.

◆

As we started the court case, I reminded myself that I needed to protect my reputation. We collected our evidence; it included a lot of powerful evidence from British Airways' staff. Gerrard received a call from an ex-British Airways employee called Sadig Khalifa. He said that he had been told to go out and get more passengers from other airlines. He was also told to collect information about Virgin Atlantic. This included flight information: the number of passengers booked on flights, the number who went on to the aircraft, the mix between upper class and economy, and the time of departures. They were told to keep their activities secret.

I then received a call from Michael Davis, a BA director who was a friend of my parents. He asked whether we could meet. This was the first sign of an apology. Lord King and Sir Colin Marshall were clearly unwilling to meet me and admit that there was any truth in my accusations, so Michael Davis had been sent instead.

'I think the three of us – you, me and Sir Colin – should have a little chat. You see, the King is dead; long live the Marshall.'

He was telling me that Lord King's days at British Airways were over.

'If we are going to have a sensible relationship in the future, I think you, me and Sir Colin should sit down together,' Michael said.

I was listening to someone talk about somebody else's money. The BA directors would receive their salaries whatever happened. The BA shareholders would pay for Brian Basham, for the detectives and the lawyers when I sued them. But Virgin Atlantic was my company. If BA stole an upper-class passenger to New York, Virgin lost £3,000, money that we couldn't reinvest in the business. BA had tried hard to put me out of business and my staff out of their jobs. They had forced me to sell Virgin Music. I was very angry. I wanted more than a quiet meeting of gentlemen. British Airways' activities were unlawful and I wanted compensation.

I called Michael Davis and told him that I couldn't quietly let my accusations fade away. The court case would start in January and the British Airways directors would be questioned by George Carman, one of the most powerful lawyers in the country.

I felt confident that we could beat BA. We had discovered a lot about their dirty tricks, and we had also found evidence of an extraordinary BA secret operation.

Someone contacted my office with evidence about a secret operation by BA that involved various private detectives. He said that he had a computer disk containing a diary of everything the detectives had done. I arranged to meet him and I wore a hidden microphone so that I could tape the conversation.

The computer disk revealed an operation named 'Covent Garden'. It contained details of how the team of detectives persuaded some of BA's senior management that *we* were running a secret operation against BA. They estimated that we were spending £400,000 on this operation. We later found out that BA was spending £15,000 a week on Covent Garden.

On one occasion, the detectives watched a hotel in Lancashire where BA's head of publicity, David Burnside, was supposed to be meeting an 'agent' that worked for Virgin. The plan failed when Burnside failed to turn on his secret tape recorder. I could have spared BA the trouble: I have never employed private detectives and never will.

On 7 December 1992 George Carman told me that BA had withdrawn their case and paid just under half a million pounds to the court. We later found out that just before the court case was due to start, BA's lawyers told them that they had no chance of winning. If they wanted to avoid a lot of negative publicity, their only option was to make a payment into the court and negotiate an out-of-court settlement.

I wondered whether to accept the money. I could put all the BA directors into court and destroy them. Although this was tempting, it would make me appear vicious and was very risky.

'You've got to remember why you brought this case,' George Carman advised me. 'You wanted the dirty tricks to stop and to protect your reputation. BA have admitted that you are right. If you continue with the case, the jury might compensate you, but because you're a rich man they might give you less than £500,000. That would be a failure for you and a success for BA. If the jury give you less than BA have paid into court, you will have to pay the lawyers' costs. So you may win the case but lose a lot of money.'

'What do we do now, then?' I asked.

'We have twenty-one days to accept the money.'

'So we'll do that?'

'Good Lord, no,' George said, looking shocked. 'I'm not going to accept it. I'm going to make them give us at least £600,000.'

He spent a week negotiating the payment. On 11 December 1992, we agreed the terms: £500,000 to me personally for the libel and £110,000 to Virgin Atlantic.

◆

Inside the court it was very quiet. Lord King, Sir Colin Marshall and Robert Ayling weren't there. Brian Basham had gone overseas, but his lawyers were still trying to have his name removed from the statement of apology. The judge listened to their arguments, then asked British Airways' lawyers for their opinion. They agreed with Virgin that Basham's name should be included in the apology.

George Carman stood up and read the agreed statement. In it, British Airways and Lord King accepted that the comments they made about me and Virgin Atlantic were completely untrue. They apologized and agreed to compensate me. In return, I and Virgin Atlantic agreed to end the case. There was only one thing that I didn't like in their apology. The directors placed the blame on their staff and denied that they knew anything about the campaign against me. It was one statement they refused to take out.

Outside, among the journalists and photographers, I held up both hands and shook my fists in victory. 'I accept this ... not only for Virgin,' I said, 'but also for all the other airlines: for Laker, for Dan Air, Air Europe and B-Cal. They went under and we survived British Airways ...'

Back at Holland Park the party started. I decided to share the £500,000 which had been given to me among all the Virgin Atlantic staff, since they had all suffered from the pressure which British Airways had put on us.

Much later, I was talking to someone when I suddenly felt exhausted. I realized that we had won. I smiled, fell sideways and fell deeply asleep.

◆

From 1993 we had money and a strong brand name that could be lent to a wide variety of businesses. We could follow our instincts. I could have retired and learnt to paint or how to beat my mum at golf. People asked me, 'Why don't you have some fun now?' but for me, this was fun. Fun is the secret of Virgin's success.

I believe that Virgin will never stand still. When I began writing this book a couple of years ago, Virgin was not involved in many of the businesses that now take up so much of my time. A lot has happened since 1993 that reflects my ideas about life and business, but I will write about that in another book. Since 1993 Virgin has expanded perhaps more quickly than any other European company, and has developed dramatically. For now, I would like to give an idea of where Virgin is and explain some of the issues that are important in the closing years of the century.

In 1993 I had already thought about developing a range of Virgin non-alcoholic drinks, led by Virgin Cola, which could rival Coca-Cola, one of the world's top ten companies. Coca-Cola is the most profitable company in the world. It has only one competitor: Coke has 40 per cent of the American market, Pepsi has about 30 per cent. Outside the US, Coke completely dominates. But when I studied the business, I found some weaknesses and I thought that the magic of the name had been broken. There was some resistance to the project within Virgin. Understandably people wanted to protect our brand name. It was the first of many objections to using the Virgin name.

When people warn me against doing something, I grow increasingly determined to try it. We knew that our product was as good as either Coke or Pepsi, and the first tasting we had at the local school showed that most people preferred Virgin Cola to the others. Within a few months we were selling £50 million of Virgin Cola across the country. We've moved into France, Belgium and South Africa, and we've even got a Virgin Cola machine underneath the Coke sign in Times Square, New York.

We also had a lot of discussions about life insurance before we decided to set up Virgin Direct.

'Life insurance?' everyone said. 'People *hate* life insurance. You can't trust the salesmen. It's a terrible industry. It's definitely not a Virgin type of business.'

'Exactly,' I said. 'It's got possibilities.'

My instinct told me that the world of financial services was full of mystery and that there was room for Virgin to offer a simple alternative. We needed a partner who knew the industry and could provide the money to go with the Virgin name. Virgin Direct, our financial services company, started with Norwich Union as an equal partner. After we entered the industry, it was never the same again. We offered good-value products and thousands of investors rushed to buy. We set up a new office in Norwich rather than in the City.

The initial signs were good, but we realized that we were going faster and further than was comfortable for Norwich Union. After a short time we arranged for Norwich Union to sell their shares to a partner who shared our ambitions. Together with Australian Mutual Provident, we now offer some of the country's most popular financial products.

◆

Although we employ over 20,000 people, Virgin is not a big company – it's a big brand made up of lots of small companies. Every time one of our businesses gets too big, we divide it into smaller units. The results have been excellent. When we sold Virgin Music, we had fifty related record companies and none of them had more than sixty employees.

The Virgin way has been to develop many different companies and let them grow naturally. For most of our companies we have started at the beginning rather than bought existing businesses. When I start new companies, I don't have a complicated view of business. When I think about the services I want to offer on Virgin Atlantic, I imagine whether my family and I would like to buy them for ourselves. Quite often it's as simple as that.

Of course, life becomes more complicated. In recent years Virgin has bought companies to add to the ones it has set up. MGM Cinemas was the first big purchase we made, and we also bought two large sections of British Rail. We improved the cinemas quite quickly, but the trains will take much longer. Unfortunately, train passengers expected that as soon as Virgin took over the running of the trains, great changes would take place. It is more complicated than that. Our two train companies have 3,500 employees and we needed to build completely new trains and negotiate with Railtrack, the company that owned the railway lines, to improve the tracks and signalling. Despite the difficult start, we are confident that Virgin Rail will eventually offer a cheap, fast, efficient train service. Our new 225-kilometre-an-hour trains will reduce journey times all over the country, and their comfort and safety will make them the best trains in Europe, and possibly the world.

When you have a great product, you have to protect its reputation. My reputation has been threatened twice – first by British Airways and second by Guy Snowden. His company GTECH was behind Camelot, which runs the British National Lottery. I met Guy Snowden when the British government finally agreed to set up the National Lottery. I felt strongly that the Lottery should be run by a company that would give all the profits to charity. I asked John Jackson, with whom I had worked before on a business project, to develop our charitable bid. GTECH was the leading supplier of lottery equipment, so we met them to ask them to supply us if their own bid failed.

John Jackson and I met Guy Snowden for lunch on 24 September 1993. He didn't want to supply us with equipment, and I didn't want to join him in making a bid. Snowden pointed out that if we made a bid, it would cost

GTECH millions of pounds. They would have to reduce the percentage they were going to charge as operators from 15 to 13 per cent and possibly lower. Each percentage reduction was worth £40 million a year.

I noticed that Snowden began to sweat. He shifted in his chair and looked at me. 'How can we help you, Richard? I mean, how can we help you personally?' I was being offered a bribe.

'What do you mean?' I said, astonished and angry and trying to give him the chance to stop. But he didn't.

'Everybody needs something in life,' Snowden said.

'Thank you,' I answered. 'I'm quite successful. I only need one breakfast, lunch and dinner a day. The only way you could have helped is by providing services for our bid.'

I stood up and left the room. I did not want to be part of this man's world. We were trying to make a bid for the National Lottery that would give millions of pounds to charity. This man was trying to bribe me to let his bid succeed. This would give less money to charity and would make him and his company rich. I ran to the bathroom and wrote some of his words on a piece of paper. Then I went back upstairs and John and I showed Snowden out of the house.

'I wasn't mistaken, was I?' I asked John. 'That was a bribe, wasn't it?'

'It most certainly was,' John told me.

In the court case that followed, the jury supported me. In his final statement our lawyer, George Carman, said that a reputation for honesty is more important than any commercial success. As he said, Guy Snowden had 'picked the wrong man, said the wrong thing in the wrong place at the wrong time'.

◆

Although I have enjoyed a lot of success in my business career, my family is the most significant thing in my life. It is the strength of my family which has given me the courage to attempt my balloon flights, and kept me struggling with my business projects.

I spend much time travelling, and value the moments when the family is together. In many ways we are closest when we are all on Necker. I look at Holly and Sam and realize that I don't want to plan their lives for them. I just want them to be happy. At the moment Holly wants to be a doctor and Sam wants to climb trees and rescue cats. I know that other businessmen like Rupert Murdoch and Robert Maxwell made their children read business reports before breakfast, but I don't want that.

As we relax together on Necker Island, I know that our original plane is flying from Heathrow to JFK. She's been flying from London to New York since 1984. Other Virgin planes are flying to South Africa and Hong Kong. The audiences have left the Virgin Cinemas, but there will be queues outside Heaven nightclub. The Japanese and Paris Megastores are shut, but late afternoon crowds will be looking through the CDs at the New York Megastore before buying a can of Virgin Cola.

Each of those projects was a step into the unknown – like losing one's virginity. But unlike really losing your virginity, in whatever world you make for yourself you can keep doing new and different things. That's what I have always wanted for Virgin. I wouldn't want it any other way.

Business Wordlist

bankrupt   in a state of financial ruin

board   a group of people who manage, advise or watch over a company

bond   a contract document promising to repay money borrowed by a company, often with **interest**

capital   money and property used to start a business or to produce more wealth

corporate   relating to a large company, or **corporation**

currency   money, in coins and notes, which is used in a particular country

equity   the value of a property or of a company's shares; **equities** are shares that give you some of the profits

interest   payment received by a lender for the use of their money, or paid by a borrower

merge   to join together into one company

negotiate   to try to come to an agreement with another person through discussion

network   a system which connects people, organizations or things together

objective   a business aim

option   a contract giving a right to buy or sell at a particular price in a certain period

retail   the sale of goods to customers

return   the profit or income from an investment

security   something that you promise to give someone if you cannot repay money borrowed from them; **securities** are investments in stocks and shares

share   one of the equal parts into which ownership of a **corporation** is divided

speculate   to take a business risk in the hope of a gain

stock   investments in a company, represented by shares or fixed interest securities; goods available for sale or distribution

underwrite   to accept financial responsibility for something

ACTIVITIES

Chapters 1–3

Before you read

1 What products or services do you know of that have the Virgin brand name? Name some of the Virgin products that are available in your country.

2 Find the words in *italics* in your dictionary, then answer these questions.

    a If you write an *autobiography*, who will you write about?

    b What is the title of your favourite *album*?

    c Is *abortion* legal in your country?

    d What is *marijuana*?

    e How does *dyslexia* affect a person?

3 Find these words in your dictionary. Use them in the sentences below.

    affair   distribute   instinct   leaflet   manor   millionaire   virgin

    a We ..... hundreds of ..... to get publicity for the event.

    b His business ..... were very good; he soon became a ......

    c They met secretly at an old ..... house, and started an ......

    d A ..... is someone who has never had sex.

After you read

4 Who

    a was Branson's best friend when he was a child?

    b set up *Student* magazine with Branson?

    c lent Branson money to help him buy the Manor?

    d offered her home as security when Branson was arrested?

5 Answer these questions.

    a How did Branson persuade advertisers to invest in *Student*?

    b What services did the Student Advisory Centre offer?

    c What difficulties caused Virgin Mail Order to lose money?

    d In what ways were the first Virgin record shops different to other high street record shops?

6 Describe how Richard Branson broke the law. Why did he do it? What happened to him? What decision did he make after the event?

Chapters 4–6

Before you read

7 The music industry is very profitable and millions of records are sold every day. Discuss why music is so important to people. What types of music do you like to listen to?

8 Find the words in *italics* in your dictionary. Are these statements true or false?

   a If you are made *redundant*, you are given a job.

   b If you own the *copyright* of a book, you get *royalties* every time a copy is sold.

   c On a CD, an album has one song and a *single* has many songs.

   d A *catalogue* lists a range of products.

   e A *jubilee* is a celebration of a special event.

   f A *gay* person has relationships with people of the same sex.

After you read

9 Where

   a did Richard Branson first meet his second wife, Joan?

   b is Necker Island?

   c did the first Virgin Airways flight take off from and land?

   d was the first Virgin shop outside London?

10 What

   a was Simon Draper's first job with Virgin?

   b was the name of Mike Oldfield's first successful album?

   c were the three negotiating aims Simon Draper and Richard Branson developed when signing contracts with bands?

   d caused Nik Powell to leave Virgin?

11 Who were The Sex Pistols? Why did they keep changing record companies? Why was Branson interested in them?

Chapters 7–9

Before you read

12 If you were setting up an airline, what services would you offer to your customers? What would persuade them to fly with you and not with another company?

13 Find the words in *italics* in your dictionary and answer the questions.

    a What is a *megastore*?

    b Who would you ask for an *overdraft*?

    c What is the main business of an *aviation* company?

    d What are *dividends*?

    e Where would you go to *sue* someone?

    f Name a company that *sponsors* sporting events in your country.

After you read

14 Why did Richard Branson

    a think that there was an opportunity for a new airline?

    b have problems with Randolph Fields?

    c decide to sell Virgin shares to the public?

15 Discuss Richard Branson's enthusiasm for dangerous sports. Why do you think he takes part in these? How could the risks he takes affect Virgin?

Chapters 10–12

Before you read

16 What do you know about the Gulf War? Find out when it took place, who was involved and what it was about.

17 Find the words in *italics* and answer the questions.

    a Describe an advertising *campaign* that has impressed you.

    b Why might a businessperson sue for *libel*? What do they hope to gain?

    c What is a *pirate*? How do pirates make money?

    d If you are asked to find a *slot* in your diary, what are you looking for?

After you read

18 How did Branson get involved in the Gulf War?

19 Who
  a is Janet Jackson and why was she important to Virgin?
  b is Lord King and how did he react to the Virgin flights to Iraq?
  c is Clive Anderson and what did Richard Branson do to him?
20 Describe in your own words some of the ways in which British Airways carried out its 'dirty tricks' campaign.

Chapter 13

Before you read
21 From the information in this book and your own knowledge of Virgin products and services, discuss why the brand has become so popular and successful.
22 Check the word *lottery* in your dictionary. Why do people enter lotteries? Why do many people decide not to play?

After you read
23 Why did Virgin sell Virgin Music? How did this sale affect Branson and the other directors of the Group? Why?
24 Why does Virgin continue to expand into new products and services?
25 'Our lawyer, George Carman, said that a reputation for honesty is more important than any commercial success.' Do you agree with this statement? Discuss why honesty is important in business and how you would react if you were offered a bribe.

Writing

26 After reading his autobiography, what opinions have you formed of Richard Branson? Write a brief assessment of the man, his achievements and his business philosophy.
27 This book is adapted from Richard Branson's official autobiography, *Losing My Virginity*. Why do you think Branson chose that title for his book?
28 Write a newspaper report about the British Airways 'dirty tricks' campaign. Describe some of BA's activities, why they took this action and what Branson did to stop them.

29 Why is Branson attracted to dangerous sports like hot-air ballooning? Write about some of his sporting adventures and the dangers he has faced.

30 Give your opinions of this book. Do you think it gives a balanced picture of Branson and his achievements? Which parts did you particularly enjoy? Would you recommend this book to other readers? If so, why?

31 Describe a business that you would like to set up. What services or products would you offer? Would it be a small business or a large one? How would you make it successful?

Answers for the Activities in this book are available from your local Pearson Education office.
Alternatively, write to: Marketing Department, Penguin Longman Publishing,
80 Strand, London WC2R 0RL.
Also visit www.penguinreaders.com for your free Factsheet for this book.